THE WORLD'S
WILD PLACES

We must go through a natural revolution if we are to survive on Earth.
We need to change people's perceptions.
If there's no environment, there's no human race.
We are in a state of global denial.

Ted Turner

The future: to our children, our grandchildren and yours.

Colin Prior

COLIN PRIOR

THE WORLD'S
WILD PLACES

CONSTABLE • LONDON

CONSTABLE & ROBINSON

3 THE LANCHESTERS

162 FULHAM PALACE ROAD

LONDON W6 9ER

WWW.CONSTABLEROBINSON.COM

FIRST PUBLISHED IN THE UK IN 2006 BY CONSTABLE, AN IMPRINT OF
CONSTABLE & ROBINSON LTD

REPRINTED 2006

A COPY OF THE BRITISH LIBRARY CATALOGUING IN PUBLICATION DATA
IS AVAILABLE FROM THE BRITISH LIBRARY.

ISBN-13 978-1-84529-350-5

ISBN-10 1-84529-350-9

CONTENTS

FOREWORD

I first met Colin Prior at the World Wilderness Congress (which grew out of a suggestion by my friend Magqubu Ntombela in the Imfolozi Game Reserve in 1976) in Alaska, where I had just delivered the keynote address. Colin showed me some of his photography of Scotland, and it set my veins pulsing. Each image transported me in heart and mind to the Highlands, the glens and the islands.

The same ability characterizes this volume of photographs of the world's wild places. Each image transports one, inwardly and outwardly. From the humpback whale spouting in the Denmark Strait in ethereal morning sunlight, to the view of a river in the Samburu National Reserve, they contain that brooding mystery of wild places which draws the sensitive soul and the modern traveller who understands that there is such a phenomenon as a spirit of place.

Behind the photographs also lies a great depth of understanding, a sense of the joy of discovery as well as dark intimations of the future. Not only has Colin Prior captured the mood of the land, but he has intuitively and brilliantly grasped the ecological perils that face all life on our planet.

One particular image, of the solitary and magnificent black rhino standing in the shadow of a deep depression, tells the world a sad story. In the 1950s – at a time when we were working to save the southern white rhino from extinction – there were an estimated 70,000 black rhino in Africa. Now that number is 6,000. Similarly, where once there were over 2,500 of the northern white rhino in the former Belgian Congo, Uganda and the Sudan, now barely 20 survive in the Garamba National Park. For the last black rhino and northern white rhino to survive the unrelenting poaching onslaught, will require the help of the world.

These then are the world's wild places; but everything portrayed – landscape, seascape, rivers, animals, fish and birds – is under threat. George Schaller's description of what it will mean to the mountain if the snow leopard becomes extinct sums it up: *'The mountains will remain magnificent even without wildlife but when the last snow leopard vanishes from the icy crags, an intangible aura of mystery will vanish too.'*

I appeal therefore to everyone who reads and looks at this book to support the conservation of all national parks and wild places. They enshrine the sanity of our world.

Dr Ian Player
Founder of the WILD Foundation
and the World Wilderness Congress

INTRODUCTION

Anyone picking up this book with its marvellous array of pictures might on first glance think that the world was still as full of wild places as it has been in human memory and history. They would be wrong.

The insidious growth in human population, the spread of cities in which more than half our species now lives, the increasing exploitation of resources to feed our consumer culture, the impacts of climate change, and the resulting pollution of land, sea and air worldwide, are together changing the surface of the Earth in a manner summed up in the title of a recent book by John McNeill *Something New Under the Sun*. In 1877 the poet Gerard Manley Hopkins could already write of the world wearing man's smudge and sharing man's smell. Since then the smudge and the smell have reached even further, and few wild places are now free of them.

Yet their value to us has in no way diminished. Nor has the threat which encroachment on them represents to the Earth's ecosystems as a whole. All this was well brought out in the Millennium Ecosystem Assessment of 2005. It is relatively easy to make the case for action to mitigate or adapt to the effects of climate change. In the words of the British Government's Chief Scientific Advisor, climate change is the biggest threat we face, bigger even than terrorism. But to make the case for protection of specific wild places or for conservation in general is much more difficult.

There are four main factors – ethical, aesthetic, economic and ecological – which should drive our thinking. They all need to be evaluated in terms of the pressure which comes from people wanting to exploit wild places, particularly equatorial forests, for short term human benefit. We also have to reckon with the redistribution of heat and cold, rain and drought, and extreme climatic events to be expected this century.

First, and most difficult to convey, is the ethical and spiritual dimension. Do we have the right, however defined, to exterminate so many other species on the living planet whether they are of use to us or not? Should we be causing what has been called the sixth extinction in the geological series of extinctions in Earth history? This is not a point which caused Christianity much concern in the past. There have been honourable exceptions, but most Christian thinkers have seen humans as separate from the rest of nature which they believed was for their plunder or pleasure. However, respect for life as such has always been a central tenet of Buddhism and Taoism, among other systems of belief. There is an increasing awareness that humans have some kind of ethical responsibility for the welfare, or at least the continued existence, of our only known living companions in the universe.

A point also ignored is the extent to which we are composite creatures. The vast majority of cells in our bodies are not our own. They belong to bacteria or other micro-organisms. We cannot even breathe or digest our food without their help. The degree of our dependence on other organisms is of a complexity beyond measurement. The ethics of respect for nature is tightly linked to the ethics of respect for ourselves.

The second major factor is the aesthetic. The aesthetic aspects of nature usually go without saying, but they are hard to define. There is, I believe, a profound human instinct which causes people to feel linked to the natural world. Even the most hardened city dwellers need space and greenery in their work and play. The culture of every people is closely allied to its landscapes and their inhabitants, and cannot be dissociated from them. The sheer wonder of nature touches and inspires us all, whether in the clear night skies of the desert, or on mountain tops, or in the living exuberance of the tropical forest. All this is demonstrated in this volume.

The third major factor is economic. Ethical and aesthetic arguments are of enormous, indeed primal, importance for the psychological health of any society, but they are usually unpersuasive against short-term arguments of self-interest. Our economic interest in biodiversity in its wider aspects is obvious. We need to maintain our own good health as well as that of the plants and animals, big and small, on which we depend for medicine and food. We have our place in the food chain like any other creature, and are more vulnerable than most as predators at the top of it. Wild places represent a kind of reservoir of species, and insurance against disaster (for example in maintaining genetic diversity). Here our lack of knowledge is actually dangerous. As E. O. Wilson has pointed out, we do not always know which species are crucial to the wellbeing of others. Yet the loss of a keystone species is, in his words, like a drill accidentally striking a power line. It causes light to go out all over.

The last and perhaps most important factor is ecological. We enjoy, mostly without recognizing it, an enormous wealth of free natural services. Such services mean a broadly regular climatic system with ecosystems, terrestrial, marine and atmospheric, to match. We rely on forests and vegetation to produce soil, to hold it together and to regulate water supplies by preserving catchment basins, recharging groundwater and buffering extreme conditions. We rely upon soils to be fertile and to absorb and break down pollutants. We rely on coral reefs and mangrove forests as spawning grounds for fish and wetlands, and on deltas as shock absorbers for floods.

Likewise we rely on the natural processes of recycling and waste disposal. We rely upon the current balance of insects, bacteria and viruses; and we assume the health of plants and animals unless we find to the contrary. Yet few realize the extent to which we have been appropriating the resources of the Earth for our own purposes. Already we use – or abuse – some 40 per cent of total photosynthetic production on land. Nature has an importance far beyond that of a warehouse of marketable raw materials.

All this is now being put at risk. In the last two or three years the alarms have sounded and are still increasing in urgency. There have been many successful

species in the history of life. The proliferation of grass and flowing plants is a good example. But in all previous cases natural correctives have limited the effects.

So far human ingenuity has overcome most problems, particularly in the last 100 years, and our species is now multiplying at an extraordinary rate. A quick look at recent history tells a lot. The human impact on the Earth has first slowly and then rapidly increased over the last 40,000 years. Hunter gatherers fitted easily, although sometimes uncomfortably, into the ecosystems of cold and warm periods of the Pleistocene. People migrated in response to changing conditions. But farming with land clearance between 10,000 and 8,000 years ago changed everything. It may even have changed the climate and, by affecting emissions of carbon dioxide and methane into the atmosphere, halted a return to colder conditions. With a vast increase in human population came towns and eventually cities. Tribal communities evolved into complex hierarchical societies. Before the industrial revolution some 250 years ago, the effects of human activity were local, or at most regional, rather than global. Now the impact is indeed global.

The problem is almost on a geological scale. No wonder the Nobel prize winner Paul Crutzen with his colleague Eugene Stoermer should have named the current epoch the Anthropocene, in succession to the Holocene epoch of the last 10,000 years.

What then are we to expect? Are we capable of establishing a lasting relationship of mutual benefit to the living Earth and those of its unruly inhabitants who are ourselves? How are we to recognize that the last 200 years or so have been a bonanza of inventiveness, exploitation and consumption which may not continue? All successful species, whether bivalves, beetles or humans, multiply until they eventually come up against the environmental stops, reach some accommodation with nature, and willy-nilly restore some balance. In the long history of the Earth, we are the only species capable of recognizing that the problems we have created exist, and that sooner rather than later something has to be done about them.

In all this the role of wild places is critical. Perhaps the first requirement is to recognize their value, not just for humans but in and for themselves. They form an ever more critical part in the good functioning of Gaia or the Earth system as a whole, a 'single, self regulating system comprised of physical, chemical, biological and human components' (as described in the Declaration on Global Change published after the Amsterdam conference of the four great international global research programmes in July 2001).

Next we have to improve our understanding of how the ecology of wild places works in all its complexity and variability. That means thinking more widely. We have to bring in such factors as human population pressure on wild places, the demands made on them for water and raw materials, the long-distance toxic effects of human activities (as in the Arctic), and the false economics which looks for short term profit and fails to take account of long term cost. Over the last few years stock market indices may have risen, but the world's natural wealth, measured by the health of its species, fell by no less than 40 per cent between 1970 and 2000.

A particular hazard for wild places is tourism. At present little of the wealth generated by tourism goes to the people who live on the spot. This means that many local communities resent tourism, and in sensitive environmental areas have little incentive to protect and conserve their surroundings. They sometimes feel imprisoned in a kind of zoo. If local people are to identify themselves with the good health of their own environment, then they must see most of the return from it.

At present most fees charged for admission to national parks or other areas of conservation are derisory. They scarcely cover the most elementary requirements of conservation. In a way tourists rent other people's environments for brief periods, and should be ready to pay a fair price for them. This in turn requires stronger local control. Nothing is more important than control of numbers. This can be done relatively easily in such isolated places as the Galapagos Islands, Machu Picchu in Peru, or Bhutan in the Himalayas, but control elsewhere has often been ineffective. The recent Millennium Ecosystem Assessment concluded that 60 per cent of the ecosystem services evaluated were either being degraded or being used unsustainably.

Some of those who will read and enjoy the pictures of this book will be keen to see the wild places for themselves. I hope they will do so. As a traveller myself, I ask only that they show due reverence and awareness of the threat to wild places. I end as I began with Gerard Manley Hopkins:

What would the world be, once bereft

Of wet and wildness? Let them be left,

O let them be left, wildness and wet;

Long live the weeds and the wilderness yet.

Sir Crispin Tickell

Chairman Emeritus of the Climate Institute,

and Director of the Policy Foresight Programme

of James Martin Institute for Science

and Civilization, University of Oxford

AFRICA

They say that once you get 'bitten by Africa' it never leaves your system. How else can you explain the fascination that people from all over the world have for this diverse, astounding, stupendous continent?

I once heard Dr Ian Player offer a plausible answer. 'Africa is the "cradle of mankind",' he remarked. '*Homo sapiens* can trace our roots back five million years to Africa. Maybe there is still something of the five-million-year-old African in each of us.' I like to believe he is right. Certainly, travellers to all parts of Africa seem touched by something deep-seated and fundamental. It is not exactly their soul that responds, nor just their heart, but not their reason either. And, whatever that shared experience is, there is frequently a common denominator – the wilderness. For all its hundreds of tribes, variety of cultures, not to mention nearly a billion people, Africa still seems to represent wild spaces.

But for how long?

We know that in the Western world – Europe and the United States, and increasingly in the East as well, our concept of space is defined largely by our immediate surroundings. Our homes, our rooms, our garden, the local park, the sports field or the school. Our contact with wild places is virtually non-existent. Even our national parks are controlled environments, the products of many years of careful (or sometimes careless) management. Most wilderness areas are now accessed by made-up roads; camping grounds have amenities laid on (partly for convenience, partly to reduce the cumulative impact of our short summer vacations on the land). The mobile phone provides instant and virtually guaranteed contact with the world we seek (for that brief spell) to leave behind.

But that is not yet the case in many parts of Africa. It is hard to appreciate the sheer scale of the continent. A national park the size of Wales or Israel, a forest the size of France, a swamp the size of Switzerland. We have a perception of great swathes of land still untroubled by human interference or activity. And as for that other distinctive feature of the African landscape, the wildlife, we think of wild animals living in abundance in wild areas. We like to preserve these illusions – sadly, however, they are no longer always the reality.

Take a look at the real map, not the one from a geography text book, which seems to indicate that the greater Congo forest extends almost from the shores of central west Africa to the Tanzanian border or that the east African savannah stretches for as far as the eye can see. No, not that map. The real map shows logging concessions running into millions of hectares, mining concessions, hunting concessions, ranches of two million hectares or more. It shows the urban sprawl of great unplanned cities like Nairobi oozing out across the surrounding plains like a random amoeba. It shows deforestation taking place at such a rate as to make even a utilitarian European blush. After all, we took a couple of centuries at least to demolish the old forests that used to cover much of western Europe. Kenya has lost 90 per cent of its natural forest cover in just forty years.

Yet there are still wild places, secret strongholds that the human tide has yet to reach. Take Kora National Park in northeast Kenya. At over 500 square kilometres (200 square miles), it is modest for Africa but would rank as one of the largest parks in Britain. And unlike protected areas in many other countries, which are places where people live too, Kora is home to only animals.

Some argue that such an exclusive concept sows the seeds of Kora's ultimate demise: keeping people out fosters resentment, and one day the policy will have to change. Others look at Kora's delicate thorn-and-bush ecosystem, its erratic semi-desert rainfall pattern and its fragile soil structure, and envisage what would happen if the doors were opened and settlement occurred. It would be a matter of a few years before unrestrained livestock, charcoal burning and subsistence agriculture took their inevitable and fatal toll. Kora would no longer be a wild place – it would not be fit for any life, human or animal.

Keeping places like Kora unspoilt is not easy. Huge herds of goats, cattle, sheep, and camels to the north spill out of Somalia and head for the permanent waters of the Tana River. The temptation to cross, to enter Kora is great. Protecting the park as a wild place takes time and money. There are dozens, hundreds, possibly thousands of 'Koras' right across Africa. They may not be semideserts; they may indeed be forests, or plains. But they are still wild places that would suffer irreversible damage if humans were to play out their existence there.

The question is if we (and by 'we' I mean the human race) want to protect these places – why? And if we can answer that one, the next question is – how?

It seems all too easy to say that, considering the humanitarian problems with which the world is now confronted – competition for fresh water, the need for arable land, food shortages, famine, disease, corruption, and the lack of basic human rights such as education and health care; we should make these our priority and reject other considerations. People first and foremost.

No doubt those challenges indeed need addressing. Whether increased aid is the answer, or debt forgiveness or real measures to tackle climate change, or social justice and good governance, it is hard to know. I have visited villages in countries that have been the recipient of countless millions in aid, and where government ministers seem able to sustain several houses and luxury cars on their modest salary, and seen people about as poor as it is possible to be.

Would it not be easier simply to admit defeat, let the wild go to the wall, convert the parks into ranches and fields, turn the forests into dollars and, for a while at any rate, allow people to live a better life?

Easier, maybe. The answer – no.

We need wild places, room to let the spirit breathe, space to let our imagination reconnect with the five-million-year-old African inside each and every one of us. And if we acknowledge that for the sake of our sanity we must keep some of this planet wild and free, then we must find the ways to make it so.

Some say that eco-tourism is the key. Eco-tourism – horrid word that means nothing except what you want it to mean. Better to say environmentally responsible tourism, indicating that each of us has to take responsibility for the travel we make. Of course, this rubs up against the issue of air travel and climate change. There is no easy answer. Travellers are not going to stop travelling, planes are not going to stop flying, and of course tourism can, under the right circumstances, play a vital role in sustaining Africa's wilderness areas. But responsible tourism is not going to be the whole solution.

If humanity needs wild places, then we are going to have to pay for them, one way or another. The problem is not lack of money: the world is awash with money. It is building resorts in Dubai, paying for interstellar exploration, Turner masterpieces, wars across the globe ... so it is not about money – it's about will. It is probably possible to pay for the effective annual operation of all of Africa's designated national parks for about $250 million a year. That is five landscape paintings by Turner. Money talks – but only when those who hold the purse strings are willing to let it.

The next twenty-five years will, in my opinion, be critical. Either wild places will be permitted to survive, nourishing our soul, energizing our spirit, confirming our humility ... or they will dwindle and die. These photographs will then serve either to inspire us, or to remind us of what we had and lost so easily.

I hope the five-million-year-old African in you makes the right decision.

Will Travers
CEO of Born Free Foundation UK
and President of Born Free USA

left: Hunting cheetah, Masai Mara National Reserve, Kenya
right: African elephant calf and mother, Samburu National Reserve, Kenya
previous page: Koitogor and Lololowki, Samburu National Reserve, Kenya

above: Lowamara and Ololokwe, Samburu National Reserve, Kenya

right: Elephant herd, Ewaso Nyiro River, Samburu National Reserve, Kenya

previous page: Ewaso Nyiro River, Samburu National Reserve, Kenya

left: Mother and child rock formation, Matopos National Park, Zimbabwe
right: African tusker, Matusadona National Park, Zimbabwe
previous page: Lake Mtshelele, Matopos National Park, Zimbabwe

above: Black rhinoceros, Matusadona National Park, Zimbabwe

right: Leopard, Serengeti National Park, Tanzania

previous page: Lake Kariba, Matusadona National Park, Zimbabwe

above: Deadvlei, Namib-Naukluft National Park, Namibia

right: Oryx, Namib-Naukluft National Park, Namibia

previous page: Sossusvlei, Namib-Naukluft National Park, Namibia

page 30-31: Baobab, Lake Manyara National Park, Tanzania

left: Gecko and lizard tracks, Kalahari Desert, Namibia

above: Epupa Falls, Kuene River, Kaokoland, Namiba

previous page: Sossusvlei, Namib-Naukluft National Park, Namibia

left:　Petite Anse, La Digue, Seychelles

right:　Anse aux Cedres, La Digue, Seychelles

previous page:　Anse Cocos, La Digue, Seychelles

next page:　Aride Island, Seychelles

pages 46-47:　Oasis, Zafrane, Tunisia

Page 14-15

Koitogor and Lololowki, Samburu National Reserve, Kenya

Camera: Linhof 617S; lens: Schneider Super-Angulon 90mm f5.6; film: Velvia 50

The essential need to conserve Africa's remaining vital ecosystems inspired the African Wildlife Foundation to mark a new era in African conservation by establishing the African Heartlands Program. Samburu National Reserve is strategic because of its mosaic of acacia-grass-land savanna, the Ewaso Nyiro River and the elephant-migration corridors, which run through the Reserve.

Page 16

Hunting cheetah, Masai Mara National Reserve, Kenya

Camera: Canon EOS1V Mark II; lens: 70–200mm f2.8L IS

Poised to strike, this hungry cheetah stalked the continuous single-file procession of migrating wildebeest. From the cover of the long grass, it watched with intense concentration for a calf to become momentarily separated from its mother, but in vain. Wildebeest are not normally on the menu for cheetahs, owing to their size.

Page 17

African elephant calf and mother, Samburu National Reserve, Kenya

Camera: Canon EOS1V Mark II; lens: 70–200mm f2.8L IS

Finding ourselves among a herd of foraging elephants, we saw three tiny calves emerge from the undergrowth and frolic like new-born lambs, jumping on each other's backs and trunk wrestling. Mum, however, was never far away to give reassurance when required, as seen in this touching image.

Page 18-19

Ewaso Nyiro River, Samburu National Reserve, Kenya

Camera: Fuji GX617; lens: SWD90mm f5.6; film: Velvia 50

Fringed with giant acacias, figs and doum palms, the Ewaso Nyiro River rises some hundreds of kilometres to the west in the foothills of the Aberdares, and vanishes beyond Samburu in the recesses of the Lorian swamp. The river is at its best in the Reserve, broad and sluggish with a large population of crocodile, seen on sandbanks at almost every bend.

Page 20

Lowamara and Ololokwe, Samburu National Reserve, Kenya

Camera: Linhof 617S; lens: Schneider Super-Angulon 90mm f5.6; film: Velvia 50.

This area is an isolated basalt mountain with dramatic cliff faces that tower above the surrounding plain. Ol Donyo Sabache is some 30km (20 miles) northwest of Archer's Post along the main Isiolo-Marsabit road. It is often called Ololokwe, a name that refers to the general area rather than the mountain itself. Three-quarters of its 14km (9-mile) circumference is a sheer precipice up to 500m (1,650ft) high.

Page 21

Elephant herd, Ewaso Nyiro River, Samburu National Reserve, Kenya

Camera: Canon EOS1V; lens: 70–200mm f2.8L IS; film: Velvia 100

Ecologically, elephants are an essential component of the habitat. They disperse seeds and modify the vegetational landscape, creating habitats for various species. As elephants increasingly come into contact with people, however, they cause the destruction of crops and property, and even loss of life. This puts elephants and people on a collision course that must be re-routed if both are to thrive.

Page 22-23

Lake Mtshelele, Matopos National Park, Zimbabwe

Camera: Linhof 617S; lens: Schneider Super-Angulon 90mm f5.6; film: Velvia 50

The Matobo or Matopos Hills are an area of granite kopjes formed over two billion years ago as granite was forced to the surface. Over time, this has eroded to produce smooth 'whaleback dwalas' and broken kopjes, strewn with boulders and interspersed with thickets of vegetation.

Page 24

Mother-and-child rock formation, Matopos National Park, Zimbabwe

Camera: Canon EOS1N; lens: 70–200mm f2.8L; film: Velvia 50

These bizarre balancing rock formations are the result of erosion along regular fault lines in the rock. In most areas the hills are aligned in steep ridges, often densely wooded on the lower slopes, supporting numerous tribes of baboons.

Page 25

African tusker, Matusadona National Park, Zimbabwe

Camera: Canon EOS1N; lens: 24–70mm f2.8L; film: Velvia 50

This trip was my very first safari. When we walked round a hill into this huge elephant, it did not strike me as being extraordinary. It was only after a number of years and subsequent safaris that I realized what a magnificent specimen this elephant had been. Few African elephants with tusks of this size now exist in the wild, as a result of ivory poaching.

Page 26-27

Lake Kariba, Matusadona National Park, Zimbabwe

Camera: Canon EOS1N; lens: Schneider Super-Angulon 90mm f5.6; film: Velvia 50

Situated on Lake Kariba's southern shore, two thirds of this 1,500 sq km (600 sq mile) national park is accessible only by foot. Comprising wooded hills, plateau and shoreline, the park itself is most easily accessed by boat from Kariba. As I stood waiting for the sun to set, two lionesses exploded from the Mopane scrub in hot pursuit of a buffalo, and I made hasty retreat to the boat.

Page 28

Black rhinoceros, Matusadona National Park, Zimbabwe

Camera: Canon EOS1N; lens: 300mm f2.8L; film: Velvia 50

Before heading for the cover of the bush, the rhino stood momentarily in silhouette: I felt it symbolized the Rhino's Last Stand. Despite sustained efforts to control the trade of rhino products, there has been little reduction in poaching pressure on the black rhino population remaining in Zimbabwe.

Page 29

Leopard, Serengeti National Park, Tanzania

Camera: Canon EOS1N; lens: 70–200mm f2.8L; film: Velvia 50

The first time I heard the rasping cough of a leopard outside my tent door, it fairly got my attention. By day, leopards often lounge and nap in large trees such as acacias, where having successfully made a kill, they will drag the prey back up onto a convenient branch to prevent theft by lions or hyenas. They will then return to the tree for several days to feed and rest, as this one has just done.

Page 30-31

Baobab, Lake Manyara National Park, Tanzania

Camera: Fuji GX617; lens: SWD90mm f5.6; film: Velvia 50

Internationally recognized as a Biosphere Reserve, Lake Manyara National Park is one of the word's richest remaining refuges for wildlife. Amongst the baobabs and grasslands, ecological threats such as habitat fragmentation, land-use change and population growth continue to challenge biodiversity.

Page 32-33

Sossusvlei, Namib-Naukluft National Park, Namibia

Camera: Fuji GX617; lens: SWD90mm f5.6; film: Velvia 50

When we think of sand dunes, we tend to think of smooth, undulating, shape-shifting forms. However, what I discovered as I waited for the sun to rise was that they possess well-defined edges which are continually re-shaped by wind shear. Seen in this low angle of light, the delineation between light and shadow is clear, literally like a line drawn in the sand.

Page 34

Deadvlei, Namib-Naukluft National Park, Namibia

Camera: Fuji GX617; lens: SWD90mm f5.6; film: Velvia 50

Perhaps one of the most spectacular sights in Namibia is the eerie and almost other-worldly 'Deadvlei' adjacent to Sossusvlei. In its tortured beauty, it is a landscape that appears to have sprung directly from a Salvador Dali canvas, where distance and perspective become warped, and time seems to lose all relevance.

Page 35

Oryx, Namib-Naukluft National Park, Namibia

Camera: Canon EOS1N; lens: 70–200mm f2.8L; film: Velvia 50

The impressive black-and-taupe, spiral-horned oryx is master of the shadeless wilderness and is superbly adapted to arid regions. The oryx can survive with a body temperature as high as 45°C (113°F), which is usually lethal, because the animal cools blood to the brain by passing it through the nostrils first. The body temperature is allowed to rise – obviating the need to perspire, and thus conserving water.

Page 36-37

Sossusvlei, Namib-Naukluft National Park, Namibia

Camera: Fuji GX617; lens: SWD90mm f5.6; film: Velvia 50

Namibia's southern coastal park is enormous, measuring almost 50,000 sq km (20,000 sq miles) and encompassing a wide variety of different desert environments. The most dramatically beautiful of these is the Sossusvlei region, where one encounters massive, apricot-orange sand dunes that are higher than any in the world.

Page 38

Gecko and lizard tracks, Kalahari Desert, Namibia

Camera: Canon EOS1N; lens: EF 100mm f2.8 Macro; film: Velvia 50

By interpreting nature's vocabulary of footprints and foliage, San bushmen were able to pursue their quarry and build up information about the patterns of animal behaviour. These skills traditionally have been passed down through the generations orally (since few read and write), and are now in danger of being lost permanently.

Page 39

Epupa Falls, Kunene River, Kaokoland, Namibia

Camera: Fuji GX617; lens: SWD90mm f5.6; film: Velvia 50

Epupa Falls is a unique environment: the palm-fringed river is punctuated by islands of giant, statuesque baobab trees, with deeply eroded fissures in which waterfalls flow. The Namibian and Angolan governments are presently considering the development of a hydroelectric facility, which would require damming the river below Epupa Falls, displacing the local Himba people.

Page 40-41

Anse Cocos, La Digue, Seychelles

Camera: Fuji GX617; lens: SWD90mm f5.6; film: Velvia 50

The combination of pink granite, weathered into the most surreal shapes, and golden coral sands is a unique landscape found only in the Seychelles archipelago. The opportunity to capture the natural rhythms of the turquoise seas or fleets of clouds racing across cobalt skies is a challenge for the landscape photographer.

Page 42

Petite Anse, La Digue, Seychelles

Camera: Canon EOS1N; lens: 70–200mm f2.8L; film: Velvia 50

The opportunity to spend time in locations such as this is always a privilege. I find stimulation from many sources: in the shapes of the landscape, in the colours of the sea and in the sheer energy of the ocean. Trying to absorb and distil these feelings in a still image that does justice to the experience of being there is never a straightforward task.

Page 43

Anse aux Cedres, La Digue, Seychelles

Camera: Fuji GX617; lens: SWD90mm f5.6; film: Velvia 50

A shark's fin of granite, created over the aeons by the power of the sea, a source of endless fascination to me. Such formations, uniquely characteristic of this area, have been smoothed into shapes so perfect they appear to have been cast by man.

Page 44-45

Aride Island, Seychelles

Camera: Linhof 617S; lens: Schneider Super-Angulon 90mm f5.6; film: Velvia 50

Aride has one of the most important seabird populations in the Indian Ocean. Over 1.25 million seabirds regularly breed on Aride, including the world's largest colony of lesser noddies, the world's only hilltop colony of sooty terns, and the Indian Ocean's largest colony of roseate terns (named arideensis, after the island).

Page 46-47

Oasis, Zafrane, Tunisia

Camera: Fuji GX617; lens: W180mm f6.7; film: Velvia 50

Arriving before dawn, I noticed that a cloud base had established itself overnight and that any sunrise would be short-lived. However, there was a clear gap above the horizon where the sun would appear, and I set up my camera in anticipation. It lasted about three minutes, during which the sun illuminated the dunes, first in soft pastel tones and then in more direct light, and I shot three rolls.

ASIA

One quarter of our planet's land surface, including large parts of Asia, is covered by mountains. Their highest summits are both the goal of mountaineers and, in many religions, the abode of the gods. Mount Everest – also known as Sagarmatha by Nepalis and Chomolongma by Tibetans – is the ultimate aspiration for tens of millions of mountaineers; while Mount Kailash, in remote western Tibet, has a far greater importance, as the holiest of mountains for nearly a billion Buddhists and Hindus. Every year, thousands of pilgrims make a circuit around the mountain, many of them traversing the whole route on their knees.

Mountains are among the most striking symbols of wilderness. Yet, even these massive edifices of nature are surrounded by the threat of change.

On the timescale of human lives, mountains seem eternal and unchanging, but on geological timescales, they come and go. As soon as a mountain starts to rise, whether from volcanic activity or the uplift of part of the Earth's crust, chemical, physical and biological processes start to wear it down. The low mountains of the Appalachians and the Scottish Highlands may once have been as high as today's highest mountain range, the Hindu Kush–Himalaya, which continues to rise at about six centimetres (2.5 inches) a year: Mount Everest is now higher than when it was first climbed in 1953.

The fact that mountains rise high into the atmosphere, interrupting the passage of air masses and forcing them to release the moisture they hold, leads to some of their greatest benefits for both the 700 million people who live in mountain areas and many billions who live downstream. While mountain areas occupy only a small proportion of most river basins, most of the rain and snow falls in them. Cold temperatures during winter mean that moisture is stored as snow until the spring melt, when it is released to be used for agriculture both in the mountains and on the plains below. Sophisticated irrigation systems have been developed in even the driest mountain areas, such as Ladakh in far northwestern India, to make the most of this vital resource, while Pakistan's agriculture relies almost entirely on mountain water. Unfortunately, the use of mountain water in arid areas sometimes has significant environmental and human impacts – one of the worst examples being the use of water for the vast cotton fields of Central Asia, leading to the gradual disappearance of the Aral Sea.

While the highest irrigation channel is one of the most visible boundaries in many mountain landscapes, marking the upper edge of productive land, the upper forest boundary, or tree line, is often even more evident. Above this, the open tundra covering vast areas of many mountain ranges may appear wild, yet over centuries or even millennia it has been changed imperceptibly by the grazing of the domestic animals. Its lower edge has often been pushed down hundreds of metres into the forest by burning, cutting and grazing. In mountain areas around the world, the high summer pastures are an essential complement to the forests and fields below. Traditionally, mountain people have moved up and down with the seasons, making the most of the resources available at different times of the year. Only in recent decades have such seasonal patterns of use begun to break down. Sometimes this has been the result of regulation, or changing ownership and management patterns, such as those which have separated the nomadic Gaddis of Himachal Pradesh, India, from their ancestral grazing lands. Elsewhere, the driver of change has been the construction of facilities for tourism in areas previously used only by a few summer herders.

On the global scale, the highest rates of deforestation are in tropical mountain areas. There are many reasons. Harvesting for timber is frequently one of these, and is often still legal, despite logging bans such as those in China following major floods in the 1990s. Sometimes at least as important is clearing for agriculture to provide for the needs of both growing mountain populations and immigrants moving up from lower altitudes, notably as road access improves. As ever higher and steeper slopes are cleared and cultivated, and as the number of harvests taken from one field increases from one to as much as four a year, the risks of soil erosion and the depletion of nutrients grow. Yet the picture is not all negative: improved management techniques and appropriate crops can be part of the answer, as can better locally based cooperative institutions, especially for managing forests and irrigation systems.

In recent years, the need for cooperation has also been recognized as essential for the effective management of the many national parks in mountain areas. The original model for national parks was Yellowstone, where local people were excluded when the park was designated in 1872. This approach continued well into the late twentieth century in the mountains of Asia and elsewhere. However, it was usually not successful: almost always, local people had used certain resources in the designated area – such as land for grazing or plants for harvesting for medicinal purposes. In addition, as populations grew around these 'uninhabited islands', so did the pressures to use their resources. One solution is to involve local people in the management of national parks and to give them access to their natural resources in ways that are sustainable. Indigenous knowledge may indeed complement Western science in assessing the correct levels of use.

National parks are only one of the attractions for the hundreds of millions of tourists who visit mountain areas each year. The oldest form of mountain tourism is religious pilgrimage, which still brings tens of millions to the shrines of the Himalaya each year, as well as many millions to holy sites in the mountains of China, Japan and Korea. Increasingly, this takes place alongside mass tourism, which has led to huge changes in the economies of many mountain areas, as well as made a significant impact on the cultures and societies of their people.

Mass tourism too is contributing to a larger change. A major factor in the rapid rise of international tourism in mountain communities around the world has been the availability of cheap air transport. This is a major source of greenhouse gases, the cause of climate change. Mountain areas and their people are already experiencing some of the effects. Nearly all glaciers are melting, which in the short term may be beneficial to those relying on meltwater, but will cause major problems in the long term. Particularly in the Himalaya, the likely increase in the number of glacial lake outburst floods (GLOFs) may present a real danger.

Although glaciers are made of ice, lakes can form on top of them, as a result of melting by the sun; they also form beneath them, where meltwater rivers become restricted. Or lakes may be created behind the front moraine of glaciers. GLOFs occur when these lakes overflow, or when the surface water melts through to the base of the glacier. Immense volumes of water are suddenly released, often causing devastating damage and many deaths. At least twelve GLOFs have been recorded since 1935 in Tibet, and others in Nepal, including one which destroyed an almost-complete hydro-electric plant.

Another likely effect of climate change is a shift in the timing of the monsoon, which would affect many aspects of life throughout the Asian mountains. We should further recognize that climate change is not only about relatively gradual changes; as the atmosphere warms up, there will be more extreme events, such as hurricanes, windstorms, floods, and major snowfalls.

The effects of climate change in the mountains may not all be negative: benefits may include shorter winters, longer growing seasons for crops, and the possibility to grow them at higher altitudes – if the soils and weather are suitable. But one thing is now beyond doubt: mountain regions and their people are ever more influenced by externally driven processes in a world that is changing rapidly and often unpredictably.

Professor Martin Price
Director of the Centre for Mountain Studies,
Perth College, Scotland

left: Lichens on moraine, Ghondokhoro Glacier, Karakoram Mountains, Baltistan

right: Erratic, Baltoro Glacier, Karakoram Mountains, Baltistan

previous page: Central Karakoram Group, Khaplu, Baltistan, Pakistan

left: Trango Towers (5,844m), Baltoro Glacier, Karakoram Mountains, Baltistan

right: Moonrise, Chogolisa (7,665m), Karakoram Mountains, Baltistan

previous page: K2 (8,612m) and Broad Peak (8,047m), Karakoram Mountains, Pakistan

left: K2, Vigne Glacier, Karakoram Mountains, Baltistan

right: Leyla Peak (6,069m), Karakoram Mountains, Pakistan

left: Konde Ri (6,187m), Lumding Himal, Sagarmatha National Park, Nepal

above: Dudh Kosi, Phakding, Sagarmatha National Park, Nepal

previous page: Ama Dablam (6,856m), Khumbu Glacier, Sagarmatha National Park, Nepal

left: Cho Oyu (8,153m), Ngozumpa Glacier, Sagarmatha National Park, Nepal

below: Himalayan snowcock, Gorakshep, Khumbu Glacier, Nepal

above: Kangtega (6,799m), Sagarmatha National Park, Nepal

right: Himalayan griffon vulture, Tengboche, Sagarmatha National Park, Nepal

previous page: Mount Everest (8,848m) and Nuptse (7,896m), Sagarmatha National Park, Nepal

above: Tso Moriri, Rupsu Valley, Ladakh

right: Tso Moriri, Rupsu Valley, Ladakh

left: Stalactites, Ko Lao Bile, Andaman Sea, Thailand

above: Ko Poda Nok and Ko Khom, Andaman Sea, Thailand

previous page: Ko Ya La Hu Tang, Andaman Sea, Thailand

left: Ko Lao Pe, Andaman Sea, Thailand

above: Tanjung Aan, Lombok, Indonesia

previous page: Ko Pak Ka, Andaman Sea, Thailand

next page: Chocolate Hills, Bohol Island, Philippines

left: Kitayamasaki Point, Rikuchu Kaigan National Park, Japan

above: Jodogahama, Rikuchu Kaigan National Park, Japan

previous page: Kitayamasaki Point, Rikuchu Kaigan National Park, Japan

next page: Jodogahama, Rikuchu Kaigan National Park, Japan

AUSTRALASIA

For those peoples who have called themselves civilized, wild places have long been 'The Other'. Until very recently, wildernesses contained the stuff of a civilized society's nightmares: wild people, wild animals, untracked spaces. Many legends recount the story of the hero who takes a little-used path into wilderness – a desert, a forest, or mountains – finds and vanquishes the horrors there, and returns, triumphant and remade. In the hero's return, we also see the other face of wild places: they are the places where people go to regain their soul.

In our time, that ambiguous thing called human progress has largely made redundant the ancient terrors of wilderness. People of wild places, shadowy to the civilized world only because of their difference, were once a chief terror of wilderness travel. Now they have either vanished into history or been tamed. Where artefacts remain, like the ochre-ringed hand prints on countless cave walls in the red-rock ranges of Australia's outback, we feel not fear, but regret. Regret that the Aboriginal culture that may have occupied these so-called waste lands for 30,000 years is now weak or dead, and with its passing has vanished all the knowledge that made these places hospitable to people.

Nor are the spaces themselves to be as feared. While it remains possible to get fatally lost in any of the world's wildernesses, wild regions now tend to present a challenge to be overcome, rather than a perilous Hansel-and-Gretel-style encounter with the unknown. With a handheld Global Positioning System (GPS) unit, or just a good topographic map, there is less need for special knowledge or relationships to guide the adventurer through landscapes once avoided – in the case of New Zealand's rugged, rainswept Fiordland National Park, often even by the native Maori. The wealth of information on wildernesses now available would utterly amaze those who gave us the first literate descriptions of these places. Such information buffers the modern traveller from the privations of those who first sought to claim wildernesses for their peers. Such as the diet of Ernest Giles, explorer of Australia's deserts, in mid-1874:

I heard a faint squeak, and looking about I saw, and immediately caught, a small dying wallaby, whose marsupial mother had evidently thrown it from her pouch. It only weighed about two ounces, and was scarcely furnished yet with fur. The instant I saw it, like an eagle I pounced upon it and ate it, living, raw, dying – fur, skin, bones, skull, and all. The delicious taste of that creature I shall never forget.

As for the wild animals that once threatened those who ventured into wild places, they have either been hunted to extinction or, in a very recent reversal, are now the object of a visit to the wilderness. No dangerous animal still in the wild has not been extensively studied, and its haunts and habits written about and broadcast. Unless the traveller is plain unlucky – and some are – being threatened by a wild animal in a wild place is today likely to be the result of willful ignorance or recklessness. Every few years, it seems, a visitor to Australia's north gets taken by a crocodile within sight of a crocodile-warning sign.

Civilization has pursued its foes right into the world's wildernesses, and usually overcome them, but it has failed to change the nature of wilderness itself. Wildernesses tend to remain not because of foresight, but because they are inaccessible, uninhabitable, or hard to cultivate. The whole globe was once wilderness; what is left is the regions people have not found a use for, 'the wastes'. Belatedly, we are discovering that the best use for wilderness is to leave it just as it is.

Wild country has long had its Romantic enthusiasts, but real raw wilderness is acquiring a new call, once heard only by the mystic or the outlaw, as an antidote to modern life's discontents. Wild nature is the black to civilization's white. Without it, we have no calm space where we can retreat from the congestion of everyday life. The globe is becoming crowded, societies irritable. Most of us now live in cities, as far removed from nature as people have ever been. But we remain in every way creatures of nature, dependent on the soil and sunlight for our food, prey to microbes, trying to reconcile ancient biological responses with our overly sophisticated modern lives.

Jesus went into the wilderness to seek clarity; millions of people today do the same, instinctively looking for natural places to escape the clamour and conflicts that our way of living has created. Some find in wilderness just a splendid landscape, perhaps with a hint of its former menace; others discover an ineffable peace that they can't quite describe except in terms of beauty and quiet. 'The most beautiful thing we can experience is the mysterious,' Albert Einstein observed. 'He to whom this emotion is a stranger, who can no longer pause to wonder and stand rapt in awe, is as good as dead; his eyes are closed'. And the emotional effect of the day's first and last sun on a range, whether it be the ochreous purple-red cliffs of the Flinders Ranges in South Australia, or the mighty 'Lord of the Rings' landscape of New Zealand's Dingwall Mountains, remains one of life's happy mysteries.

But not all humanity regards untouched wilderness as having an intrinsic value. Exploitation of wilderness is often the last recourse for the poor and dispossessed, who need to survive after their traditional way of life has fallen to 'progress'. The less developed countries of the world can rightly point to the hypocrisy of the industrialized nations in calling for an end to the exploitation of wilderness. Most of the countries of the so-called First World have spent their histories levelling large tracts of forest, mining and grazing deserts, and damming mountain-fed rivers. And there is still clear-felling, overgrazing and species loss in these countries.

In the more affluent nations, however, people are voting in favour of wilderness. There is a slowly growing understanding that the loss of a natural environment is something that no technological cunning can ever begin to restore.

Forests are the Earth's lungs, cleaning and moistening the air that each of us inhales each minute. When a forest goes into the woodchip mills, so does part of the Earth's breathing apparatus. And when the trees disappear over vast regions, so does the rainfall that once favoured the moist outbreathing of the vegetation, leaving an area impoverished not just in its ecology but also in its climate.

Deserts denuded by ill-managed livestock rise up and march, as the Sahara rose up in response to similar abuse millennia ago; as the mighty Gobi Desert is relentlessly moving on Beijing, threatening to throw its dunes against the city within the next fifty years.

Rivers turn to mere gutters when their nutrient- and oxygen-rich snowmelt flows are regulated by concrete dams, or pollution kills the life in their waters.

Added to this toll is the crisis of global warming. The potential effects of this human-made apocalypse have long been talked about, and now the reality appears to be with us. Like the miner's canary, the wildernesses are feeling the consequences first.

As in the legends, today's wildernesses are full of signs and portents regarding our fate. Like the hero, we need the courage to read these signs – finding them is no problem – and to act. To dismiss the signs as 'out there' is to ignore that we are woven of the same stuff. As the pioneering Scottish-American environmentalist John Muir said 150 years ago: 'When we try to pick out anything by itself, we find it hitched to everything else in the Universe.'

Each generation needs to learn that the world is not made solely for their use, but that it exists and blossoms separate from self-obsessed humanity. And there is no better teacher of this principle than wilderness.

Matthew Cawood

Author of *The Australian Geographic Book of the Flinders Ranges*

left: 'The Beehives', Purnululu National Park (Bungle Bungles), Western Australia

below: Piccaninny Creek, Purnululu National Park (Bungle Bungles), Western Australia.

previous page: Piccaninny Creek, Purnululu National Park (Bungle Bungles), Western Australia.

left: Bunyeroo Gorge, Flinders Ranges National Park, South Australia

above: Red kangaroos, Flinders Ranges, South Australia

previous page: Ragged Ranges, Kimberley, Western Australia

left: Strzelecki Desert, South Australia

above: Star trails, Flinders Ranges National Park, South Australia

previous page: Cullyamurra Waterhole, Coopers Creek, South Australia

next page: Red gums, Heysen Range, South Australia

left: Mount Titiroa, Lake Manapouri, Fiordland National Park, New Zealand

above: Cirrus clouds, Fiordland National Park, New Zealand

previous page: Beech Forest, Fiordland National Park, New Zealand

left: Mount Isolation, Fiordland National Park, New Zealand

right: Sunset, Hunter Mountains, Fiordland National Park, New Zealand

left: Weathered granite, Fiordland National Park, New Zealand

below: Weathered granite, Fiordland National Park, New Zealand

previous page: Lake Gunn, Fiordland National Park, New Zealand

left: Weathered granite, Fiordland National Park, New Zealand

above: Weathered granite, Fiordland National Park, New Zealand

left: Darren Mountains, Fiordland National Park, New Zealand

right: Mount Cook/Aorak (3764m), Mount Cook National Park, New Zealand

previous page: Black Giants (1640m), Dingwall Mountains, Fiordland National Park, New Zealand

Piccaninny Creek, Purnululu National Park (Bungle Bungles), Western Australia

Camera: Fuji GX617; lens: SWD90mm f5.6; film: Velvia 50

Purnululu National Park contains the deeply dissected Bungle Bungle range. This is composed of Devonian-age quartz sandstone eroded over twenty million years into a series of beehive-shaped towers or cones, whose steeply sloping surfaces are distinctly marked by regular horizontal bands of dark-grey cyanobacterial crust (single-celled photosynthetic organisms).

'The Beehives',' Purnululu National Park (Bungle Bungles), Western Australia

Camera: Fuji GX617; lens: SWD90mm f5.6; film: Velvia 50

The Bungle Bungles are by far the most outstanding example of cone karst in sandstone anywhere in the world, and owe their existence and uniqueness to several interacting geological, biological, erosional and climatic phenomena. They have become emblematic of the park and are internationally renowned among Australia's natural attractions.

Piccaninny Creek, Purnululu National Park (Bungle Bungles), Western Australia.

Camera: Fuji GX617; lens: SWD90mm f5.6; film: Velvia 50

The dramatically sculptured structures, unrivalled in their scale, extent, grandeur and diversity of forms anywhere in the world, undergo remarkable seasonal variation in their appearance, including striking colour transition following rain. The intricate maze of towers is accentuated by sinuous, narrow, sheer-sided gorges lined with majestic Livistona fan palms.

Ragged Ranges, Kimberley, Western Australia

Camera: Fuji GX617; lens: SWD90mm f5.6; film: Velvia 50

A 'Great Barrier Reef' fringed an ancient Kimberley landmass during the Devonian period, between 375 and 350 million years ago, when a tropical sea filled the Canning and Bonaparte basins. Remnants of the reef are preserved in West Kimberley as ranges of low, rugged hills extending for 300km (190 miles).

Bunyeroo Gorge, Flinders Ranges National Park, South Australia

Camera: Linhof 617S; lens: Schneider Super-Angulon 90mm f5.6; film: Velvia 50

The Flinders Ranges form a part of a larger geological structure called the Adelaide Geosyncline, a big depression that filled with sediments from about 650 to 550 million years ago. They have become synonymous because of the Ediacara Fauna: a group of fossilized plants and animals dating to before the great explosion of complex life during the Cambrian Period.

Red kangaroos, Flinders Ranges, South Australia

Camera: Canon EOS1N; lens: 70–200mm f2.8L; film: Velvia 100

Kangaroos have long been important to the survival of Australia's indigenous peoples. Aboriginals have hunted kangaroos for tens of thousands of years, for both the meat and the skins. However, since introduction of European farming methods, kangaroo populations have increased dramatically, and they are now harvested by commercial hunters.

Cullyamurra Waterhole, Coopers Creek, South Australia

Camera: Linhof 617S; lens: Schneider Super-Angulon 90mm f5.6; film: Velvia 50

Surrounded by vast expanses of desert and arid plains, Cullyamurra Waterhole is an oasis of striking contrasts. Aboriginal carvings at the waterhole are thought to have been made around 40,000 years ago. Anthropologists suggest the distinctive markings were carved into the stone using hard, flint-like rocks. Cullyamurra is the largest waterhole in Australia, and is up to 24 metres deep.

Strzelecki Desert, South Australia

Camera: Linhof 617S; lens: Schneider Super-Angulon 90mm f5.6; film: Velvia 50

Stretching from just within the New South Wales border to its northeastern boundary at Coopers Creek, the Strzelecki Desert is an extensive dune field, which includes three wilderness areas centred on Lake Hope, Lake Callabonna and Lake Frome. The dunes grow with a mixture of sandhill wattle, needlebush and whitewood, and short-lived tufted kerosene grasses.

Star trails, Flinders Ranges National Park, South Australia

Camera: Linhof 617S; lens: Schneider Super-Angulon 90mm f5.6; film: Velvia 50

A study of Aboriginal meteorology reveals an intimate knowledge of plant and animal cycles, and the intricate connections between them. This reflects the Aboriginal philosophy that 'all things are connected', and that such subtle natural linkages can reveal much about climate and weather.

Red gums, Heysen Range, South Australia

Camera: Linhof 617S; lens: Schneider Super-Angulon 90mm f5.6; film: Velvia 50

Made famous by South Australian artist Sir Hans Heysen, who wrote: 'The Flinders region has held a "'spell"' over me – the great Red Gums in the creek beds fill me with wonder; their feeling of strength of limb, of vigour and life, suggest the very spirit of endurance.' For me this image captures the very essence of his observations.

Beech Forest, Fiordland National Park, New Zealand

Camera: Fuji GX617; lens: SWD90mm f5.6; film: Velvia 50

Southwest New Zealand is one of the great wilderness areas of the Southern Hemisphere. It is an area where snow-capped mountains, rivers of ice, deep lakes, unbroken forests and tussock grasslands produce a landscape of exceptional beauty. Recognition of the area's outstanding natural values was granted by UNESCO in 1990, with the formation of the Southwest New Zealand World Heritage Area.

Mount Titiroa, Lake Manapouri, Fiordland National Park, New Zealand

Camera: Canon EOS1Ds Mark II; lens: 70–200mm f2.8L IS ISO 250

Reaching a height of 1,000m (3300ft), Fiordland's forest clings to steep faces of hard rock covered by only a thin layer of rich, peaty humus and moss. Silver beech trees dominate, with rich under-storey shrubs that include tree ferns, mosses and lichens. Thirty-five plant species are endemic to Fiordland, most of them above the tree line.

Page 111

Cirrus clouds, Fiordland National Park, New Zealand

Camera: Canon EOS1Ds Mark II; lens: 24–70mm f2.8L IS ISO 100

Forming above 6,000m (19,700ft), cirrus clouds are thin, wispy clouds that are usually blown by strong westerly winds aloft into streamers known as 'mares' tails'. Composed of ice crystals that originate from the freezing of super-cooled water droplets, cirrus generally occurs in fair weather and points in the direction of air movement at its elevation.

Page 112

Mount Isolation, Fiordland National Park, New Zealand

Camera: Canon EOS1Ds Mark II; lens: 70–200mm f2.8L IS ISO 100

Fiordland's ecosystems are threatened by introduced predators and competitors – red deer, rats, mustelids and possums prey on birds and bird eggs. Red deer compete for food with the endangered takahe, the largest living member of the rail family, and damage their habitat. The species recovered slightly after deer control was implemented, but even so, only about 130 birds remain in Fiordland.

Page 113

Sunset, Hunter Mountains, Fiordland National Park, New Zealand

Camera: Canon EOS1Ds Mark II; lens: 70–200mm f2.8L IS ISO 50

Human activity has been limited in Fiordland, but there were always some who were willing to endure adversity in the search for new places or resources. European settlement was hampered by the steepness of the terrain, isolation and the wettest climate in New Zealand. Early Maori people hunted birds here, caught fish from the sea and gathered jade from the rivers.

Page 114-115

Lake Gunn, Fiordland National Park, New Zealand

Camera: Fuji GX617; lens: SWD90mm f5.6; film: Velvia 50

Looking much as it would have done at the end of the last ice age 10,000 years ago, the region has retained spectacular glacial landforms. Rising above the surrounding 2,000m (6,600ft) Fiordland peaks, the sun has illuminated the peaks of Melita (1,680m/5,510ft) and is beginning to warm the surface of Lake Gunn.

Page 116

Weathered granite, Fiordland National Park, New Zealand

Camera: Canon EOS1Ds Mark II; lens: 70–200mm f2.8L IS ISO 50

Standing like giant chess pieces on a 1,700m (5,580ft) mountain summit, these granite forms have been eroded, over the millennia, into fantastic shapes. It's difficult to accept that they are entirely the result of natural processes, endless freeze-and-thaw cycles and wind blast, when they seem such compelling sculptures. Named the 'Transformer Man', he is a monument to time.

Page 117

Weathered granite, Fiordland National Park, New Zealand

Camera: Canon EOS1Ds Mark II; lens: 24–70mm f2.8L IS ISO 50

The oldest rocks in the region, which contain fossils some 500 million years old, were uplifted about 350 million years ago. The intense forces involved created very hard, crystalline igneous and metamorphic rocks (gneiss and granite) that are relatively resistant to erosion. I named this sculpture 'Whale Rock', and I was drawn to its simplicity.

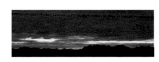

Page 118

Weathered granite, Fiordland National Park, New Zealand

Camera: Canon EOS1Ds Mark II; lens: 70–200mm f2.8L IS ISO 50

These rock formations reminded me of the shapes and textures of the granite rocks on the island of La Digue in the Seychelles. In some ways, they seemed to me like an upland version, where the enveloping turquoise Indian Ocean had been replaced with a sea of silver beech forest. Had time permitted, I would have explored this summit extensively.

Page 119

Weathered granite, Fiordland National Park, New Zealand

Camera: Canon EOS1Ds Mark II; lens: 24–70mm f2.8L IS ISO 50

Again, in this image of 'Tripod Rock', we have to remind ourselves that this structure is the result of natural processes and not the efforts of an alien life-form. Receding glaciers and erosion by wind, rain and ice are the agents responsible.

Page 120-121

Black Giants (1,640m), Dingwall Mountains, Fiordland National Park, New Zealand

Camera: Fuji GX617; lens: W180mm f6.7; film: Velvia 50

Seen from a high camp at the head of Breaksea Sound, the rising sun illuminates a cloud canopy over the Dingwall Mountains. Having been flown in by helicopter and dropped on the mountain top the previous day, I noticed an unusual crater near the summit, which I thought at first to be an excavation. Closer inspection confirmed that it was the result of a lightning strike.

Page 122

Darren Mountains, Fiordland National Park, New Zealand

Camera: Canon EOS1Ds Mark II; lens: 70–200mm f2.8L IS ISO 200

The lush rainforest carpeting the lower slopes of the mountains gives way to the incredibly steep, glacier-carved slopes and waterfalls in the Darren Range. Surrounded by snow-capped mountains, sheer rock walls plunge over a thousand metres to the sea at Milford Sound. The fjord features numerous waterfalls, and is home to dolphins, fur seals and penguins.

Page 123

Mount Cook/Aorak (3,764m), Mount Cook National Park, New Zealand

Camera: Canon EOS1Ds Mark II; lens: 24–70mm f2.8L ISO 100

With three main peaks rising from a summit crest over one mile long, Mount Cook at 3,764m (12,345ft), is the highest mountain in New Zealand. The glaciers are extensive, wrapping the entire mountain in ice: the biggest is the Mount Tasman Glacier. The mountain's isolated location near the west coast makes it vulnerable to sudden storms, which are often long and severe.

SOUTH AMERICA

A toss of a coin in 1494 sealed the Treaty of Tordesillas between Spain and Portugal, the two largest maritime powers of the time. With a signature, the two countries declared themselves the rightful conquerors of the vast lands across the Atlantic, and forever divided the personality of a continent between Spanish-speaking countries and Portuguese-speaking Brazilians. When the cultural and religious costumes of the conquering nations were merged with native indigenous cultures, South America became a wonderful mosaic of traditions that differ widely from country to country. The fate suffered by the abundant biological and mineral resources of the region, however, was tragically uniform throughout the region.

What happened over the next 300 years is painfully familiar throughout South America. It is a tale of conquest, warfare, over-exploitation, slavery, disease and political intrigue. The landscape that greeted the new arrivals is only remembered through the written accounts they left behind, because by the time a wave of independence wars swept through the continent in the early 1800s, most of the more accessible biomes and many of the indigenous cultures had been transformed forever.

Today, there are just a few remaining large tracts of wilderness left in South America, notably the Amazon, the Pantanal, and Patagonia. Most of the once immense ecosystems of the continent are now reduced to what Conservation International calls 'hotspots'.

To qualify as a hotspot, a region must meet two criteria: it must contain at least 1,500 species of vascular plants (so, more than 0.5 per cent of the world's total) as endemics, and it has to have 30 per cent or less of its original vegetation (extent of historical habitat cover) remaining. There are 25 hotspots in the world and collectively they hold as endemics no less than 44 per cent of the world's plants and 35 per cent of terrestrial vertebrates (mammals, birds, reptiles and amphibians) in an area that formerly covered only 11.8 per cent of the Earth's land surface. Their land area has been reduced by 87.8 per cent of its original extent, and thus this amazing wealth of biodiversity has been restricted to only 1.4 per cent of Earth's land surface.

South America as a whole has five such hotspots: the tropical Andes, the Tumbes-Chocó-Magdalena, the Atlantic forest, the Cerrado and the Chilean winter-rainfall Valdivian forests. Together, these areas covered an original extent of 5.5 million hectares (21,000 square miles); today there are only 1 million hectares (4,000 square miles) of intact vegetation left. And yet, collectively, the South American hotspots harbour a total of 74,892 species of plants, of which 32,100 are endemic to the hotspots. There are also 1,375 species of mammals, 184 of them endemic; 4,387 species of birds, 872 endemic; 1,507 reptiles, 527 endemic; and 2,128 amphibians, 1,034 endemic.

With a population estimated at 371 million, South America's conservation challenges continue to mount. Take for example the case of the Mata Atlântica of Brazil as a typical example of most coastal development in colonial South America. The assault on Brazil's tropical forests began shortly after the first landing by Pedro Alvares Cabral in 1500 in the southern part of Bahia, in the heart of the Atlantic forest region. The coastal forests did not yield gold or silver, but the Portuguese quickly found something else of value in them. Brazil wood or pau-Brazil (*Caesalpina echinata*) was traded for large cattle herds. This trade encouraged migration far inland along the major navigable rivers to set up cattle ranches. Later, sugar plantations became predominant along the coast of northeastern Brazil, resulting in the widespread and almost total destruction of the forests of the region. Forest burning was common practice, both to displace hostile Indian tribes and to create pastureland.

By the eighteenth century, cattle-ranching on a grand scale was the main activity throughout most of the region and sugar cane, and cattle dominated the agricultural economy until the early nineteenth century, when coffee production was greatly expanded. Increasing population also resulted in a growing demand for fuel, principally charcoal and firewood. With the establishment of the steel industry in the early 1900s, the demand for charcoal grew dramatically. From 1920 to 1940, 50 per cent of the forests of the state of Minas Gerais were destroyed for this purpose, and were replaced with what are now the most extensive eucalyptus plantations on Earth. Other locally important products also had an impact, one example being cocoa, which was concentrated in the biologically rich southern portion of the state of Bahia.

Today pressure continues. Sao Paulo and Rio de Janeiro, two of the three largest cities in South America, are located only about 400 kilometres (250 miles) apart in the central portion of the Atlantic forest region, and at least two-thirds of Brazil's population now lives in the region. These two cities, together with Belo Horizonte, Salvador and Recife, account for more than 50 million people, leading to huge demand for agricultural land, as well as industry to provide employment.

The Atlantic forest today is a highly endangered series of ecosystems, where only a tiny fraction of the original forest cover remains. The destruction has been especially severe in the low-lying coastal region and in the narrow strip of forest in the long-exploited northeast, where less than one per cent of original primary forest remains. However, it has also spread onto the foothills and slopes of the Serra do Mar, which used to be much less accessible. As a result, only seven per cent of the original natural vegetation remains intact in the region as a whole.

At the other end of the conservation spectrum are wilderness areas. According to Conservation International these are areas that are at least 10,000 square kilometres (3,860 square miles), have fewer than five people per square kilometre and have at least 70 per cent of their historical habitat intact. There are 24 areas around the world that satisfy these criteria, and eight of those are in South America. South America's wilderness areas include Amazonia, the Magellanic rainforests, the Chaco, the Llanos, the Pantanal, the Bañados del Este and Patagonia. Together, these wilderness areas cover approximately 18 million square kilometres (7 million square miles), and only 30 million people live in them, of which 9.5 million live in urban areas.

Not all these wilderness areas harbour the same amount of biodiversity, so in order to establish some conservation priorities biodiversity data was added to the analysis. Using information on the diversity and endemism of plants and four groups of vertebrates, the analysis found Amazonia to be the only High Biodiversity Wilderness Area in South America. Amazonian rainforests harbour 40,000 species of plants, of which 30,000 are endemic. They also have 425 species of mammals, 172 endemic; 1,300 species of birds, 263 endemic; 371 species of reptiles, 260 endemic; and 427 species of amphibians, 366 endemic.

The High Biodiversity Wilderness areas are important priorities not just because of their biodiversity value, but because they are facing higher threat, and our failure to act now could result in such regions rapidly becoming biodiversity hotspots within a very short space of time.

Wilderness regions, in general, have great value to humanity for the essential ecosystem services that they provide and for their benefits to human well-being. Wilderness preservation alone, however, will not be enough to conserve the bulk of our planet's biodiversity. Conservation efforts must remain firmly targeted on the hotspots, which are characterized by high threat and high biodiversity; and should be complemented by interventions first in those wilderness regions that are high priorities for biodiversity conservation, in particular Amazonia.

Despite the tremendous challenges we face in South America, there is plenty of reason for hope. There are a number of very successful conservation projects taking place, and progress is clearly been made in the creation and enforcement of protected areas throughout the continent. However, conservation challenges continue to pick up speed and there is no time to be wasted. If we focus our efforts on those regions where most biodiversity is found first, we still have a great opportunity to conserve the bulk of South America's magnificent cultural and biological diversity for the benefit and enjoyment of generations to come.

Russ Mittermeier
President of Conservation International
Cristina Mittermeier
Executive Director of the International League of Conservation Photographers

left: Lake Pehoe, Torres del Paine National Park, Patagonia, Chile

above: Black-necked swans, Torres del Paine National Park, Patagonia, Chile

previous page: Lake Pehoe, Torres del Paine National Park, Patagonia, Chile

left: Rio Grey, Torres del Paine National Park, Patagonia, Chile

above: The Horns of Paine, Lago Nordenskjold, Patagonia, Chile

previous page: Cerro Almirante Nieto and Los Cuernos del Paine, Lake Pehoe, Patagonia, Lake Pehoe

below: Lincancabur and Juriques, Atacama Desert, Chile

right: Volcán Lascar, Atacama Desert, Chile

previous page: Perito Moreno Glacier, Los Glaciares National Park, Argentina

left: Rio Tarabo, Bolivar State, Venezuela

below: Rio Tarabo, Bolivar State, Venezuela

previous page: Rio Tarabo, Bolivar State, Venezuela

page 140-141: Valley of the Moon, Atacama Desert, Chile

above: Macal River, Vaca Plateau, Cayo District, Belize

SOUTH AMERICA

Page 128-129
Lake Pehoe, Torres del Paine National Park, Patagonia, Chile

Camera: Fuji GX617; lens: SWD90mm f5.6; film: Velvia 50

Uplifted during the mountain-building process, granite intrusions in dark sedimentary rock caps are a feature of many of the mountains in this cordillera. They are characteristic of the strange landforms Patagonia is known for throughout the world.

Page 130
Lake Pehoe, Torres del Paine National Park, Patagonia, Chile

Camera: Canon EOS1N; lens: 24–70mm f2.8L; film: Velvia 50

Driven by powerful katabatic winds, williwaws send billowing clouds of spray hundred of metres into the air as they stream across Lake Pehoe. Westerly winds flow up and over the southern Andes, descending to meet the flat pampas below – the falling airmass behaves like an avalanche, gathering speed as it goes.

Page 131
Black-necked swans, Torres del Paine National Park, Patagonia, Chile

Camera: Canon EOS1N; lens: 70–200mm f2.8L IS; film: Velvia 50

Black-necked swans, such as these flying above the surface of Lago Nordenskjold, have a fairly stable population within the National Park. In the past, these swans were hunted for their down, used in the manufacture of insulated clothing and for food. Habitat loss through drainage of marsh and wetland areas continues to be the largest threat to this species.

Page 132-133
Cerro Almirante Nieto and Los Cuernos del Paine, Lake Pehoe, Patagonia, Chile

Camera: Fuji GX617; lens: SWD90mm f5.6; film: Velvia 50

Scoured out by glacial ice, this compact chain of spectacular granite spires and rock walls is separated from the ice-cap by a deep forested valley, while in the south it rises sheer from rolling steppes, scattered with lakes of all sizes. In some areas small glaciers reach the forests of Patagonian evergreen beech.

Page 134
Rio Grey, Torres del Paine National Park, Patagonia, Chile

Camera: Canon EOS1N; lens: 24–70mm f2.8L; film: Velvia 50

Swollen by glacial meltwater, the Rio Grey plunges in a waterfall over sedimentary rocks.
At these austral latitudes, spring is an ephemeral season, during which incessant storms deliver precipitation, contributing to the creation of vigorous evergreen forests and boggy moorland.

Page 135
The Horns of Paine, Lago Nordenskjold, Patagonia, Chile

Camera: Fuji GX617; lens: W180mm f6.7; film: Velvia 50

Towering above Lago Nordenskjold and Lake Pehoe, these giant granite spires are often hidden in thick cloud, appearing only occasionally before being enveloped once more. Photographed at dawn, this vertical world is illuminated by a seemingly extra-terrestrial light.

Page 136-137
Perito Moreno Glacier, Los Glaciares National Park, Argentina

Camera: Fuji GX617; lens: SWD90mm f5.6; film: Velvia 50

Although small compared with the 300km (190-mile) long ice field, the Moreno Glacier is probably the most active in Patagonia, frequently carving ice into the waters of Lago Moreno. The glacier was named after Francisco Perito Moreno, the early Argentine explorer of the Andes.

Page 138
Lincancabur and Juriques, Atacama Desert, Chile

Camera: Canon EOS1V; lens: 70–200mm f2.8L IS; film: Velvia 50

Located at the boundary of Chile and Bolivia, the Lincancabur volcano hosts the highest and one of the least explored lakes on Earth. Lincancabur is still warm, and the lake sits in the caldera at its peak. It is ice-covered most of the year but the water temperature at the bottom remains above freezing. These conditions make Licancabur a unique analogue to ancient Martian lakes.

Page 139
Volcán Lascar, Atacama Desert, Chile

Camera: Canon EOS1N; lens: 24–70mm f2.8L; film: Velvia 50

Located on the southern edge of the Chajnantor plain and to the East of the Salar de Atacama, Volcán Lascar is the most active stratovolcano in the central Andes, with an active fuming crater. At 5,641m (18,500ft) above sea level, and an edifice height of approximately 1,400m (4,600ft), it is considered a high dry volcano. Frequent eruptions have been recorded since the mid-nineteenth century.

Page 140-141
Valley of the Moon, Atacama Desert, Chile

Camera: Fuji GX617; lens: W180mm f6.7; film: Velvia 50

The Atacama is probably the driest desert in the world. While some areas of the Atacama along the coast have succulent plants like cacti, the more arid parts have no vegetation. These regions do not even have cyanobacteria – the green photosynthetic microorganisms that live in rocks or under stones in most other deserts. The desert itself is thought to be ten to fifteen million years old, making it the oldest desert on Earth.

Page 142-143
Rio Tarabo, Bolivar State, Venezuela

Camera: Linhof 617S; lens: Schneider Super-Angulon 90mm f5.6; film: Velvia 50

From a highpoint above the forest canopy, the Rio Tarabo winds its way through the rainforest – a natural break in the dense vegetation. Such is the competition for light beneath the canopy that every conceivable centimetre is occupied. Moments before, two scarlet-and-green macaws had flown above the tree tops, their crimson plumage contrasting vividly with the green foliage.

Page 144
Rio Tarabo, Bolivar State, Venezuela

Camera: Linhof 617S; lens: Schneider Super-Angulon 90mm f5.6; film: Velvia 100

Photography in tropical regions is never straightforward. Apart from high rainfall, humidity, and low light, there are myriad insects, which want either to eat you, or you to host the birth of their offspring. Shooting in a rainforest is like working inside a giant cabbage – everywhere and everything is green.

Page 145
Rio Tarabo, Bolivar State, Venezuela

Camera: Canon EOS1N; lens: 70–200mm f2.8L; film: Velvia 50

Travelling upstream to the highlands by dug-out canoe, we were afforded the best place from which to observe wildlife. Bird-life was prolific, and we observed: scarlet-and-green macaws, mealy parrots, oropendolas, toucans and, at one point, a rare harpy eagle swooping from one side of the river to the other, clutching prey in its talons.

Page 146
Macal River, Vaca Plateau, Cayo District, Belize

Camera: Canon EOS1N; lens: 24–70mm f2.8L; film: Velvia 50

The upper stretches of the Macal River extend into a remote and seldom seen area that drains the Vaca Plateau watershed and much of Chiquibul National Park. Above 760m (2,500ft), granite rock formed from molten intrusions, and there is now a landscape of great pine forests, canyons and valleys, water-falls, and vistas of stunning beauty.

NORTH AMERICA

In the early twenty-first century, it is easy to lose sight of the important role that nature and wilderness play in our lives. A growing number of people live in settings far removed from wilderness, where the connection between nature and human existence is increasingly difficult to identify. Indeed, for the first time in the Earth's history, as of late 2005, more than half the global population lived in cities.

The vast majority of city dwellers rely on market economies and modern infrastructure to provide food, water, shelter, and other necessities of life. Nature and natural processes seem to have little to do with their existence. In the developed world, this disconnection with wilderness extends beyond urban settings, probably because the key resources essential for human survival are found in stores and taps, or are available with the touch of a button or the flip of a switch. Given the conveniences available to many, it is difficult to imagine how a collection of naturally occurring plants and animals living in wild settings has much to do with daily existence. And yet wilderness, and the diversity of life found in it, is essential to human survival.

All life on Earth relies on the services naturally provided by ecosystems – plant, animal, and micro-organism communities that interact as functioning units. Ecosystem services include processes that provide essential resources such as food and water, regulate threats such as floods and diseases, and support nutrient cycling such as replenishment of soil fertility.

Living outside wild settings, we sometimes find it difficult to conceive of how people rely on nature and its services. And yet the massive damage sustained by the city of New Orleans in August 2005 from Hurricane Katrina, largely because the wetlands were no longer functioning and thus able to mitigate the floodwaters, bears witness to the importance of such services and the cost of compromising them. In the absence of disasters, nature and its services subtly benefit people all over the world. For instance, terrestrial and ocean ecosystems absorb much of the carbon emitted by human activities, helping to slow global climate change. A range of wild animals provides billions of dollars worth of pollination to fruit, vegetable,

and tree crops annually, helping to maintain the food production upon which we all rely. And nature serves as a source of medicines that benefit much of humankind, some of the best-known examples including quinine and artemisinin to treat malaria, paclitaxel to treat a variety of cancers, and several antibiotics (e.g. penicillin, tetracycline) to treat bacterial infections.

As more natural habitat is converted for human use, and more ecosystems are lost, both the range and magnitude of ecosystem services decline accordingly – increasing human vulnerability to natural disasters, infectious disease, famine and other maladies that nature has quietly protected us from for thousands of years.

Conscious efforts to maintain ecosystems help connect the natural and built environments, in the process providing an indication of how important the services of such ecosystems can be in the daily lives of people far removed from wilderness. Perhaps no single example is so evident of this than the steps taken by New York City to maintain the natural habitat of its sources of water. In the 1990s, New York decided to invest what appeared to be an enormous amount of public funds – about $1.5 billion – to protect these watersheds, buying key tracts of land, improving waste treatment infrastructure in watershed communities, and helping farmers to reduce pollution. Through taking steps to protect its sources of water, instead of opting for the usual solution of contamination followed by conventional water treatment, the city avoided the need to construct an enormous filtration plant at an estimated cost of $6–8 billion, in the process providing high-quality water for domestic, industrial, and public use by more than nine million people. Other cities in the United States (e.g. Portland, Oregon), have followed the New York example in investing to protect the watersheds where urban water supplies originate, the natural processes of filtration and purification greatly reducing the cost of water treatment prior to public consumption.

Although we can measure the benefits of the wilderness in such terms as the value of fish harvested, the volume of contaminants removed from the atmosphere and the variety of nutrients returned to the soil, wild places also provide important emotional benefits that suggest an innate, almost spiritual connection between humankind and nature. This connection is what the biologist E. O. Wilson calls 'biophilia', the human affinity for life and lifelike forms that causes people to identify with living organisms and develop attractions to certain natural settings. One can find evidence of this deep-seated connection with nature in psychological experiments.

Despite the emotional connection that people maintain with wilderness and nature, and our reliance on nature's services for many necessities of life, human demands on Earth's resources increasingly jeopardize nature and the diversity of life. Biologists estimate that plant, animal, and micro-organism species are currently disappearing at rates a thousand or more times higher than those of the past, placing the Earth on a course of mass extinction of a magnitude seen only a few times in the planet's history, and greatly endangering the ecosystems upon which we all rely. Species loss is largely a consequence of converting natural habitat to other forms, to help support an enormous human population.

The numbers in many ways tell the tale. In early 2005, nearly 6.5 billion people inhabited the Earth – more than twice the number in existence less than fifty years earlier. Currently, it takes only slightly more than a decade to add another billion people to the global population, with about 220,000 added daily to the total number of people living on Earth. During the final two decades of the twentieth century, the land used for agriculture increased on average by 130,000 square kilometres (50,000 square miles) per year, often involving the conversion of natural habitat. Although growth of population and human demand will not continue forever, researchers anticipate the addition of another 2.6 billion people, and a doubling of agricultural production, before these variables level out sometime around the middle of this century.

The challenges that face wild places have never been greater. But thanks to scientific advances in understanding our world, neither has humankind's ability to identify key concerns and design solutions to address them. Conserving natural areas that provide opportunities for people to interact with wilderness and maintain the services essential to human well-being requires careful planning. It is necessary to consider these issues alongside economic and other development goals. Such conservation begins with existing protected areas, such as national parks and other types of reserves, where ecosystems and the diverse collection of organisms that compose them continue to function.

As the global impact of human beings increases, so too must the area set aside for conserving nature. If 'corridors' of land combining human activities with natural habitat connect protected areas, then conservation expands from a series of isolated localities to integrated networks. These networks provide larger territories for those components of ecosystems that need them. And guiding development to minimize impacts on key ecosystem services maintains those services for current and future generations.

Implementing such solutions often will require difficult choices, particularly in the face of poverty, where converting nature for human use seems to provide more immediate solutions than conserving it. But given the important role that nature plays in human existence, on both emotional and practical grounds, the future of the world requires solutions that meet development goals and reduce poverty while maintaining essential ecosystem services, along with the wild places and biological diversity that provide them.

L. J. Gorenflo

Director of the Human Dimensions of Biodiversity Program

for the Center for Applied Biodiversity Science

at Conservation International

left: Foraging grizzly bear, Denali National Park, Alaska

below: Willow ptarmigan, Denali National Park, Alaska

previous page: Mount Denali, Denali National Park, Alaska

left: Moose family, Denali National Park, Alaska

below: Fall reflections, Cantwell, Alaska

left: Beaver with willows, Wonder Lake, Denali National Park, Alaska

right: Fall colours, Kodiak Island, Alaska

page 156: Mount Brooks and Mount Silverthorne, Denali National Park, Alaska

page 157: Pioneer Ridge, Mount Denali, Denali National Park, Alaska

left: Brown bear swimming, Uganik River, Kodiak Island, Alaska

below: Brown bear fishing, Uganik River, Kodiak Island, Alaska

above: Golden Eagle, Uganik River, Kodiak Island, Alaska

right: Brown bear fishing, Uganik River, Kodiak Island, Alaska

below: **Floatplane, Uganik Lake, Kodiak Island, Alaska**

right: **Kodiak National Wildlife Refuge, Kodiak Island, Alaska**

above: Three Sisters, Monument Valley Tribal Park, Arizona

left: Mitten Buttes, Monument Valley Tribal Park, Arizona

previous page: North Window, Monument Valley Tribal Park, Arizona

above: Castle Butte and East Mitten Butte, Monument Valley Tribal Park, Arizona

right: South Rim, Grand Canyon National Park, Arizona

previous page: Totem Pole and Yei Bichei Rocks, Monument Valley Tribal Park, Arizona

left: Chiricahua National Monument, Arizona

above: Echo Canyon, Chiricahua National Monument, Arizona

previous page: Turret Arch from North Window, Arches National Park, Utah

Page 150-151

Mount Denali, Denali National Park, Alaska

Camera: Hasselblad X Pan II; lens: 30mm f5.6; film: Velvia 50

Denali is an Athabascan word meaning 'High One', and at 6,100m (20,010ft) Mount Denali, also called Mount McKinley, is the tallest mountain in North America. Denali is part of the Alaska Range, a series of mountains formed from the interaction of the Pacific and North American plates. These mountains tend to have granitic cores, though some are made up of Jurassic and Cretaceous sedimentary rocks.

Page 152

Foraging grizzly bear, Denali National Park, Alaska

Camera: Canon EOS1Ds Mark II; lens: 70–200mm f2.8L IS ISO 400

Grizzly bears are omnivorous, eating a mixed diet of grasses, berries, roots, fish and small mammals. During August and September, the inland grizzlies of Denali feed predominantly on berries (up to 30,000 a day), roots and the occasional arctic ground squirrel. They are also predators of caribou and moose, and their calves.

Page 153

Willow ptarmigan, Denali National Park, Alaska

Camera: Canon EOS1Ds Mark II; lens: 300mm f2.8L IS + EF1.4X Converter ISO 400

Blending perfectly with the Denali autumn foliage and early snows, the willow ptarmigan's plumage changes colour with the seasons, turning white during the winter months and then brown in summer. The bird's ability to survive from predators using camouflage is highly evolved.

Page 154

Moose family, Denali National Park, Alaska

Camera: Canon EOS1Ds Mark II; lens: 70–200mm f2.8L IS ISO200

Having tracked this Moose family for an hour across the tundra, I anticipated where they might next go, and placed myself on a high point overlooking the Alaska Range. The autumn colours were at their peak, the tundra maroon with blueberries, punctuated with the red-orange of dwarf birch. Suddenly the family walked right into my frame, stopping to survey the way ahead.

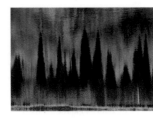

Page 155

Autumn reflections, Cantwell, Alaska

Camera: Canon EOS1Ds Mark II; lens: 300mm f2.8L IS ISO 400

On an overcast morning I managed to find a corner of a lake where the reflection was not being affected by the wind. Through a 300mm lens, I could see patterns emerging between the pinks and greens of the foliage and I shot this image, inspired by Monet's impressionistic paintings of water lilies.

Page 156

Mount Brooks and Mount Silverthorne, Denali National Park, Alaska

Camera: Canon EOS1Ds Mark II; lens: 70–200mm f2.8L IS ISO 50

Lying to the west of Denali, Mount Brooks (3,639m/11,935ft) and Mount Silverthorne (4,029m/ 13,215ft) rise like an island surrounded by a sea of ice. The Brooks and Muldrow glaciers in the west and south, and the Ruth and Traleika glaciers in the north and east, complete the ring of ice. The contrast with the golden aspens in the foreground gives some sense of the sheer scale of these mountains.

Page 157

Pioneer Ridge, Mount Denali, Denali National Park, Alaska

Camera: Canon EOS1Ds Mark II lens: 70–200mm f2.8L IS ISO 50

Photographed here at dawn, Pioneer Ridge is a long, serrated knife-edge that extends from Denali's north face. It is a direct but challenging route to the summit, where hanging glaciers, snow and ice at 70 degrees and vertical rock pinnacles need to be overcome. The route was first attempted in 1912, but was not successfully completed until 1961.

Page 158

Beaver with willows, Wonder Lake, Denali National Park, Alaska

Camera: Canon EOS1Ds Mark II; lens: 300mm f2.8L IS ISO 400

During the fall, beavers spend much of their time gathering willows, cottonwood and aspen branches, which they use to build an underwater food cache, located within a protective moat. In winter, when the rivers and lake become frozen, beavers stay warm in their lodges with an underwater food supply. A beavers' ability to change the landscape is second only to humans.

Page 159

Fall colours, Kodiak Island, Alaska

Camera: Canon EOS1Ds Mark II; lens: 70–200mm f2.8L IS ISO 100

Through the open window of a floatplane, en-route to Uganik Lake, I captured the autumnal colours of the birch trees in Kodiak National Wildlife Refuge. Established in 1941 to preserve and protect the pristine habitat of the brown bear and other wildlife. The refuge comprises more than two-thirds of Kodiak Island and a small portion of Afognak Island.

Page 160

Brown bear swimming, Uganik River, Kodiak Island, Alaska

Camera: Canon EOS1Ds Mark II; Lens: 300mm f2.8L IS + EF1.4X Converter ISO 400

Most brown bears are active during the morning and early evening hours, however during the late summer and fall months, when they are fattening ahead of hibernation, brown bears may be active throughout the day. As food become scarcer, they will travel from alpine food sources to estuaries, from berry patches and to salmon spawning sites, when its particular food source is available.

Page 161

Brown bear fishing, Uganik River, Kodiak Island, Alaska

Camera: Canon EOS1Ds Mark II; lens: 300mm f2.8L IS + EF1.4X Converter ISO 200

During September bears spent most of their waking hours feeding on sockeye and sliver salmon in an effort to build up their fat reserves in preparation for hibernation. Brown bears have a more diverse social structure than other bears owing to the close proximity in which they live. Camping discretely on the riverbed, we tried to minimise our impact on the feeding bears and observed from a respectful distance.

Page 162

Golden Eagle, Uganik River, Kodiak Island, Alaska

Camera: Canon EOS1Ds Mark II; lens: 300mm f2.8L IS + EF1.4X Converter ISO 200

With the concentrations of fish in the river estuary, it was not uncommon to see five or six bald eagles and occasionally a golden eagle. In Alaska, the range extends as far north as the Brooks Range, with a limited and scattered distribution in the southeast and rare occurrences in the Aleutians and Alaska Peninsula. Not all eagles migrate but most go south when food supplies decline.

Page 163

Brown bear fishing, Uganik River, Kodiak Island, Alaska

Camera: Canon EOS1Ds Mark II; lens: 300mm f2.8L IS + EF1.4X Converter ISO 400

Kodiak bear populations are healthy and productive. They enjoy pristine habitat and well-managed fish populations. In most areas the number of bears is stable, and in some places bear density is actually increasing. The increase of tourism, however, in some areas is impacting negatively on behavioural patterns, most notably on their ability to feed and to move freely about their territories.

Page 164

Floatplane, Uganik Lake, Kodiak Island, Alaska

Camera: Canon EOS1Ds Mark II; lens: 70–200mm f2.8L IS ISO 100

There are less than 130km (80 miles) of public roads on Kodiak Island, of which 30km (19 miles) are paved. De Havilland Beaver seaplanes have become the local wilderness taxi, and are able to transport five people and equipment into remote areas, to fish, hunt or explore. Each year up to 50 million salmon return to Kodiak streams to spawn.

Page 165

Kodiak National Wildlife Refuge, Kodiak Island, Alaska

Camera: Canon EOS1Ds Mark II; lens: 24-70mm f2.8L IS ISO 100

Scalloped and sculpted by ice, these mountains are home to populations of deer, elk, mountain goat, and snowshoe, which are now highly valued by sport and subsistence hunters. Some of these also are a source of management concern because of their potential to influence the quality of native fish and wildlife habitats.

Page 166-167

North Window, Monument Valley Tribal Park, Arizona

Camera: Fuji GX617; lens: SWD90mm f5.6; film: Velvia 50

Surrounded by empty desert, the isolated red mesas and buttes of Monument Valley provide perhaps the most enduring and definitive images of the American West. The valley represents the last remnant of the sandstone layers that once covered the entire region.

Page 168

Mitten Buttes, Monument Valley Tribal Park, Arizona

Camera: Fuji GX617; lens: SWD90mm f5.6; film: Velvia 50

Deserts that existed at the end of the Permian era 260 million years ago formed the Canyon De Chelly and Wingate sandstone that make up the buttes, totems and mesas in Monument Valley. A significant period of desertification took place during the Jurassic period, 208 to 144 million years ago, and the resulting Sahara-like desert eventually hardened into beautiful, pink Navajo sandstone.

Page 169

Three Sisters, Monument Valley Tribal Park, Arizona

Camera: Canon EOS1N; lens: 70–200mm f2.8L; film: Velvia 50

Sandstone spires have been eroded into distinctive shapes by the 'exfoliation' process, whereby the sides of the mesas are sheared off and crumble into rubble. At regular intervals there are tremendous mountains of sculpted rock with monoliths and cliff formations that bear such descriptive names as the Three Sisters, the Bear and Rabbit, and the Thumb.

Page 170-171

Totem Pole and Yei Bichei Rocks, Monument Valley Tribal Park, Arizona

Camera: Fuji GX617; lens: SWD90mm f5.6; film: Velvia 50

As early as the fourteenth century, San Juan Band Paiutes frequented the area as temporary hunters and gatherers. They named it 'Valley or Treeless Area Amid the Rocks' and vested the landscape with supernatural qualities and mythological stories. Totem Pole Rock is said to have been a god held up by lightning, and El Capitan a sky-supporter.

Page 172

Castle Butte and East Mitten Butte, Monument Valley Tribal Park, Arizona

Camera: Fuji GX617; lens: W180mm f6.7; film: Velvia 50

The origins of plant and animal fossils found in Navajo Sandstone continues to be the subject of debate. Some observers suggest that the creation of ephemeral lakes from monsoon storms were responsible for sustaining local flora and fauna. Others speculate that, as mountains in distant areas were slowly uplifted from the sea, the region became part of a huge floodplain.

Page 173

South Rim, Grand Canyon National Park, Arizona

Camera: Fuji GX617; lens: W180mm f6.7; film: Velvia 50

Although rocks exposed in the walls of the Grand Canyon are geologically old – those at the bottom are close to two billion years old – the Canyon itself is geologically young, having been formed five or six million years ago. Erosion by the Colorado River, together with that of rain, snowmelt and tributary streams, continue this process.

Page 174

Delicate Arch, Arches National Park, Utah

Camera: Fuji GX617; lens: SWD90mm f5.6; film: Velvia 50

Entrada Sandstone forms the base and pedestals of this world-famous, freestanding arch, while the Moab Member of the Curtis Formation forms the bridge. The contact between the two is a plane of weakness along an unconformity. Delicate Arch has a horizontal span of about 10m (33ft) and a vertical span of 14m (46ft). The top of the arch stands 16m (52ft) over the base.

Page 175

Delicate Arch, Arches National Park, Utah

Camera: Fuji GX617; lens: SWD90mm f5.6; film: Velvia 50

Deposited in coastal dunes during the middle Jurassic, Entrada Sandstone is the main constituent of most of the arches in Arches National Park. During the late Cretaceous and early Tertiary, the sedimentary rocks were folded into a gentle anticline and fractured into joints, which were enlarged and eroded during colder and wetter episodes of the Pleistocene.

Page 176-177

Turret Arch from North Window, Arches National Park, Utah

Camera: Fuji GX617; lens: SWD90mm f5.6; film: Velvia 50

The first stage in the development of the arches is fracturing along parallel joints. Weathering attacks the lower, more sheltered parts of the fins and creates arches. North Window is in a largely intact fin, believed to have been deposited by the wind in a vast coastal desert about 150 million years ago, during the Jurassic period.

Page 178

Chiricahua National Monument, Arizona

Camera: Linhof 617S; lens: Schneider Super-Angulon 90mm f5.6; film: Velvia 50

Like Easter Island figures and chess pieces, these pillars and spires have been eroded over millions of years, from the rhyolite tuff. Water and ice seeped into the soft zones and ate away rock particles, creating larger spaces between the blocks and ultimately leading to the landscape we see today.

Page 179

Echo Canyon, Chiricahua National Monument, Arizona

Camera: Linhof 617S; lens: Schneider Super-Angulon 90mm f5.6; film: Velvia 50

Geologic processes formed the spectacular scenery in the Chiricahua National Monument. Clouds of red-hot ash, pumice, rock fragments and gases were ejected violently from a volcano about 26.9 million years ago. This mixture fused together, compacted and cooled to form rock. Subsequently, weathering processes caused this to disintegrate and decompose along vertical joints.

EUROPE

When I was a schoolboy in the 1960s, a globe was produced in a geography lesson showing our world comprising some simple geophysical features: green splodges for the continents, separated by the blue for the oceans, and with two white caps on the bottom and the top – the polar ice caps. This was our planet.

But if I live to 100, the northern ice cap that floats on the Arctic Ocean above Europe, now three metres (ten feet) thick, is likely to have shrunk to the point of non-existence by the end of each summer. That is a profoundly alarming planetary-scale change. And what is the big deal about losing this cap? Well, much of the ice cap is covered with snow, which has the highest reflectivity of all surfaces on our planet, sending about 85 per cent of incoming solar energy back up into space. The ice cap's disappearance will reveal the open water of the Arctic Ocean beneath it, which reflects only 15 per cent of solar energy, thereby enabling a 70 per cent increase in heat absorption by this ocean.

So what we are witnessing now is the removal of one of the planet's largest protective heat shields – a vital geophysical feature holding in balance the entire global system of ocean currents, which are inextricably linked with Earth's atmospheric circulations and thus our weather patterns. This balance will be completely distorted if the shield melts away, creating, for example, new rainfall regimes, and thus affecting water supply for agriculture and urban areas, in surprisingly short time-frames of perhaps not even decades but years, followed by the inevitable attempted migrations of populations to more sustainable climatic environments. What we are considering here is an entire, unique and minimally understood ecosystem covering 3 per cent of the Earth's surface being corrupted and destroyed within our lifetime, which leaves those who care about the world we pass on to our children and grandchildren aghast.

My personal experience of the disappearing ice cap came in spring 2003, when I trekked solo to the North Geographic Pole. In places I had to crawl and smash my way through melting ice, and even at times swim across open water, towing my sledge modified to double up as a boat. I had found it necessary to introduce new techniques and equipment to enable my progress due north and

it included the development of a lightweight immersion-suit which I could wear over my polar boots and clothing, and an inflatable rim around the gunwales of my sledge to enable it to float with greater buoyancy and stability.

The explorers who follow in my tracks will be using sledge-boats, which will soon become more canoe and less sledge, to make the increasing number of thin ice and open water crossings less time-consuming and problematic. Not many people know that the first non-icebreaker boat, a Russian ship, has already reached the North Pole, navigating its way through open waterways in the summer. Over the next fifteen to fifty years, there will be so much open water in the late summer-times on the Arctic Ocean that people will be able to go on yachting holidays to the Pole.

So why is the ice cap melting? The United Nations Intergovernmental Panel on Climate Change (IPCC), made up of the world's leading Earth system scientists, concluded in its seminal 2001 report that the prime reason is human activity in the form of greenhouse gas emissions from the combustion of fossil fuels – coal, oil and natural gas.

The most significant in this cocktail of gases is carbon dioxide, which made up 280 parts per million (ppm) in the Earth's atmosphere in 1750, before the Industrial Revolution. Today it comprises 381ppm, which is higher than at any time in the past 800,000 years, including the last eight inter-glacial periods, when the globe's average temperature was eight to ten degrees warmer than during the glacial periods. This concentration of 381ppm may actually prove to be the highest in the last 55 million years.

The reason the scientists are so fixated about the concentration of carbon dioxide in our atmosphere is that analyses of ice cores in Antarctica over the last 800,000 years demonstrate beyond all reasonable doubt that carbon dioxide levels and average global temperatures are inextricably linked. The lines on the graphs follow each other so closely that it is often hard to know which is which. So when we know global carbon dioxide levels are already exceptionally high and about to escalate to heights the Earth may not have experienced for hundreds of millions of years, you can see why the scientists are increasingly desperate to let us know where we are currently heading.

Professor Bert Bolin, founding chairman of the IPCC, has said that 450ppm is probably the maximum 'safe' limit beyond which the concentrations will unleash a chain of events that will be catastrophic for the biosphere – the zone in which all life on Earth exists.

We are rapidly moving towards that maximum level with yearly increases currently of 1.5ppm. Many people are now of the opinion that we have already exceeded a safe limit. And to make matters worse, we are on the verge of a massive escalation in carbon emissions as India, China, Mexico, Brazil, Russia and South Africa accelerate their industrial output. The average global temperature rose by 0.6°C (1°F) in the twentieth century, but the IPCC expects it to rise between 1.4°C (2.5°F) and 5.8°C (10.4°F) by 2100, which will bring rises in sea levels that will effect tens of millions of people worldwide living in low-lying coastal regions.

However, we should be aware of the aggressive action now being undertaken, led by energy companies, with the support of sponsoring nations with their eye on national fuel supply strategy. There are some who are already rubbing their hands with glee at the short-term economic opportunities offered by the shrinking of the ice cap, which will enable access to previously unextractable reserves of natural gas and oil. Armadas of research vessels are now mapping the seabed of the Arctic Ocean. Russia, Norway, Canada, the United States (via its Alaskan territory) and Denmark (via Greenland) are the combatants, and their battles are being fought in the United Nations' corridors of power as they claim ownership rights, under the 'Law of the Sea', to their continental seabeds. Meanwhile, fleets of newly designed oil and gas-carrying supertankers are under construction to ship these fuels via the new trade shipping routes which will be opening up around the Arctic Ocean as its ice cap recedes – notably the Northern Sea Route and the Northwest Passage.

The irony that global warming, caused by fossil fuel use, is now making more fossil fuel accessible will not be lost on many.

So does all this mean that the game is over? Should we now just confine ourselves to relying on technology and human ingenuity to tackle each problem as it arises? What difference can we as individuals make?

The answer to these awkward questions is simply that it would be grotesquely irresponsible to bury our heads in the desert sand. The climate change process will be rampantly out of control if we wait long enough for technological solutions to be prompted by significant human suffering in our own 'advanced' countries.

As an individual, I am not a 'dark green'. But I have switched our electrical supply so that it comes from renewable energy sources, I use the trains far more than I used to – and we plan to install insulated windows in our old house. Like many, I am considerably more aware with each passing month of how my purchasing actions, large and small, have a negative impact on our planet's essentially finite resources, processes and systems. We are almost all in the more developed and advanced countries 'users' with a horrendous 'addiction' to fossil fuels – and we need to understand and accept this and wean ourselves off the habit if we are to bottom out our production of carbon dioxide. It is going to involve some 'cold turkey', but blaming big business and government is a form of denial that it is us, all of us, that have, and are, the problem.

Ultimately, the key to success really does lie at the governmental level. However, politicians always look to the short term, and are frightened by voter reaction against the sort of economic measures required to bring about the necessary scale and speed of the mass human behavioural changes – namely taxation, incentives and penalties. So it is up to us to start by making those simple changes at home, and to forge a consensus of public opinion that will give our politicians the confidence to act.

Pen Hadow

Polar explorer

left: Midnight sun, Krokhammartinden (731m) and Seiltinden (731m), Lofoten Islands, Norway

below: Rostadtindan (710m), Kjerk Fjorden, Lofoten Islands, Norway

previous page: Midnight sun, Ternnestinden (690m), Lofoten Islands, Norway

left: Old Man of Storr, Trotternish Ridge, Isle of Skye, Scotland

above: Carsaig Cliffs, Ross of Mull, Isle of Mull, Scotland

previous page: Earth shadow, Liathach (1,054m) and Beinn Eighe (1,117m), Glen Torridon, Scotland

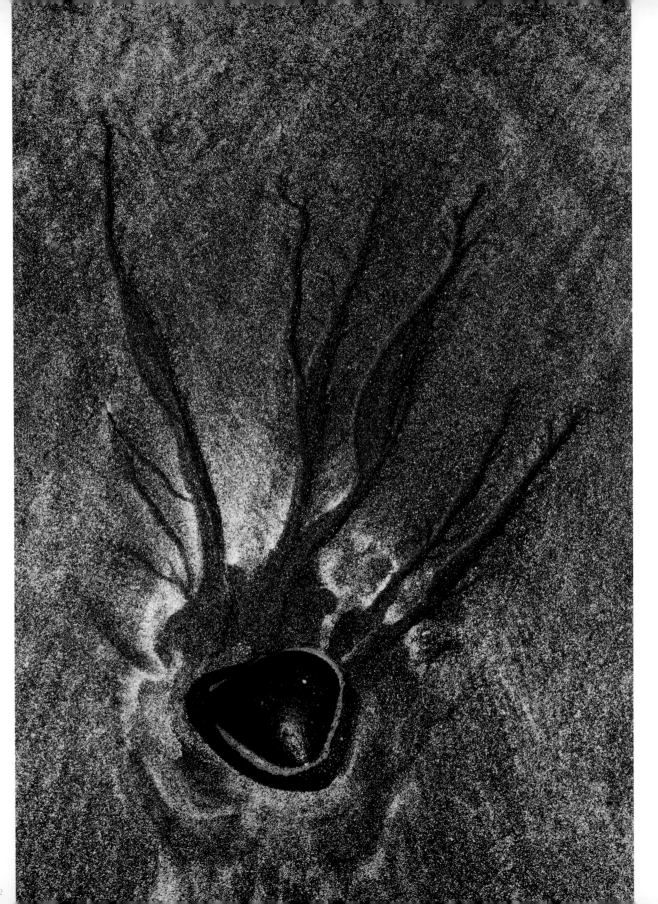

left: Stone and sand, Carsaig Bay, Ross of Mull, Isle of Mull, Scotland

right: Laig Bay, Isle of Eigg, Small Isles, Scotland

next page: Canisp (846m) and Suilven (731m), Assynt, Highland

left: Svartifoss waterfall, Skaftafell National Park, Iceland

right: Basalt columns, Aldeyjarfoss, Sprengisandur, Iceland

previous page: Aldeyjarfoss, Sprengisandur, Iceland

left: Vestrahorn, Lonsvik, Eastern Fjords, Iceland

above: Dettifoss Waterfall, Jökulsá á Fjöllum River, North Thingeyjarsysla District, Iceland

previous page: Jökulsárlón, Breidamerkursandur, Iceland

left: Icebergs, Denmark Strait, East Greenland

below: Icebergs, Denmark Strait, East Greenland

previous page: Icebergs, Denmark Strait, East Greenland

left: Humpback whale, Denmark Strait, East Greenland

below: Humpback whale, Denmark Strait, East Greenland

left: Icebergs, Denmark Strait, East Greenland

right: Polar ice, Denmark Strait, East Greenland

below: Fata Morgana, Denmark Strait, East Greenland

right: Icebergs, Denmark Strait, East Greenland

Page 184-185

Midnight sun, Ternnestinden (690m), Lofoten Islands, Norway

Camera: Fuji GX617; lens: SWD90mm f5.6; film: Velvia 50

Having climbed to the summit of Navaren (697m/2,286ft) in the late evening, the sun was low on the horizon and veiled by static cloud. I set up my camera on the tripod and retired to my sleeping bag, anticipating the sun re-appearing. At exactly 2.00am, I was awakened by the sun on my face and by this inversion, which had materialized overnight, illuminated by the most magic light.

Page 186

Midnight sun, Krokhammartinden (731m) and Seiltinden (731m), Lofoten Islands, Norway

Camera: Canon EOS1N; lens: 24–70mm f2.8L; film: Velvia 50

The Lofoten and Barents Sea areas are among the last relatively pristine marine habitats on Earth. Millions of seabirds nest and breed in this ocean area, and numerous species of fish and marine mammals are to be found living in these waters. The region, however, is under threat from over-fishing, risk of oil-tanker accidents and the oil industry's desire for new drilling grounds.

Page 187

Rostadtindan (710m), Kjerk Fjorden, Lofoten Islands, Norway

Camera: Fuji GX617; lens: SWD90mm f5.6; film: Velvia 50

The high biodiversity in the area combined with the critical life-cycle stages in many fish species in a relatively small area make the ecosystem especially vulnerable to marine pollution. All biological processes are slow, owing to the low annual average temperatures, and ecosystem recovery takes a long time after pollution incidents.

Page 188-189

Earth shadow, Liathach (1,054m) and Beinn Eighe (1,117m), Glen Torridon, Scotland

Camera: Fuji GX617; lens: SWD90mm f5.6; film: Velvia 50

After a rather cool overnight camp, I awakened to this spectacular morning and set up hoping to shoot the earth shadow. Best seen from a high elevation, the earth shadow is cast upon the atmosphere itself (purple) and is bounded above by the (pinkish) anti-twilight arch, reddened by the atmosphere and scattered into our line of sight.

Page 190

Old Man of Storr, Trotternish Ridge, Isle of Skye, Scotland

Camera: Hasselblad X Pan II; lens: 30mm f5.6; film: Velvia 50

Notwithstanding the Cuillins, the most impressive hills in Skye are in Trotternish, where the longest continuous ridge on the island has its highest point on the Storr. Below, formed by a series of landslides, which exposed the basalt lavas, the Old Man of Storr's dramatic pinnacle is a distinctive landmark.

Page 191

Carsaig Cliffs, Ross of Mull, Isle of Mull, Scotland

Camera: Canon EOS1Ds Mark II; lens: 70–200mm f2.8L IS ISO 50

Looking east from the deserted village of Shiaba, where in 1846 the landlord, the Duke of Argyll, decided that it would be in the tenants' 'best interests' if they were removed from their homes to other farms, or given passage to the New World. The time of the Highland Clearances marked a very dark period for the Ross of Mull, when many of its people were forced from the land.

Page 192

Stone and sand, Carsaig Bay, Ross of Mull, Isle of Mull, Scotland

Camera: Canon EOS1Ds Mark II; Lens TS-E 90mm f2.8 ISO 50

This stone I encountered lying on the beach amid radiating tributaries caused by the flow of a freshwater stream nearby. I visualized the image initially in black and white, but felt that its almost monochromatic qualities where enhanced by the subtle colour variation in the image. The simple graphics of the image create a powerful dynamic.

Page 193

Laig Bay, Isle of Eigg, Small Isles, Scotland

Camera: Hasselblad X Pan II; lens: 30mm f5.6; film: Velvia 50

On the shore at Laig Bay are cliffs composed of Valtos sandstone, overlain by oyster-bearing Jurassic limestone. Traversing the shore northwards are examples of dykes intruding the Jurassic sandstone, but instead of standing proud of the surrounding rocks, they have been eroded more quickly than the baked and hardened sandstone margins and form a trough.

Page 194-195

Canisp (846m) and Suilven (731m), Assynt, Highland, Scotland

Camera: Hasselblad X Pan II; lens: 30mm f5.6; film: Velvia 50

Suilven is the most westerly of the Assynt Mountains and dominates the surrounding landscape. It has the remarkable ability to change shape from different directions – from the west it appears as a great rounded dome, from the east the ridge is greatly foreshortened, and from the north and south the entire linear ridge is unfolded.

Page 196-197

Aldeyjarfoss, Sprengisandur, Iceland

Camera: Fuji GX617; lens: SWD90mm f5.6; film: Velvia 50

By far the largest of the glacier caps is Vatnajökull, in southeast Iceland, with an area of 8,300 sq km (3,200 sq miles), equal in size to all the glaciers on the European mainland put together. Rising on the north-western border, the glacial waters of the River Skjálfandafljót are heavily laden with debris, which make them turbid and yellowish-brown in colour seen here at Aldeyjarfoss.

Page 198

Svartifoss Waterfall, Skaftafell National Park, Iceland

Camera: Arca Swiss F Metric 6x9; lens: Schneider Apo-Symmar 180mm f5.6; Fuji 50

So far in Iceland, the oldest rocks dated above sea level are about fourteen million years old, and accordingly the oldest basalts are no older than the Middle Miocene, much younger than those in Britain, Greenland or the Faroes. This fits with the theory of ocean-floor spreading.

Page 199

Basalt columns, Aldeyjarfoss, Sprengisandur, Iceland

Camera: Fuji GX617; lens: W180mm f6.7; film: Velvia 50

Basaltic lava has a low viscosity and often flows for long distances from the eruption site. The lava flows are usually very thin (less than 10–30m/30–100ft) and solidify either as a ropey pahoehoe lava or as a blocky aa lava. Basalt is also very common as dykes and sills, bodies of rock that cooled near the surface in the lava conduits that once fed the lava flow.

Page 200-201

Jökulsárlón, Breidamerkursandur, Iceland

Camera: Fuji GX617; lens: W180mm f6.7; film: Velvia 50

The stunning blue-coloured lake some 300m (1,000ft) deep is the result of a combination of geological changes and glacial retreat. Glacial erosion of the bedrock and sediments has resulted in a deep scoured valley (currently beneath the ice and lake), which has simply been filled by meltwater from the glacier as the ice front has retreated.

Page 202

Vestrahorn, Lonsvik, Eastern Fjords, Iceland

Camera: Hasselblad X Pan II; lens: 30mm f5.6; film: Velvia 50

Rising to a height of 454m (1,490ft) and composed of gabbro, the Vestrahorn (West Horn) is a mountain located on the promontory between Skardsfjördur and Papafjördur. At Lonsvik, the black volcanic ash has been shaped by the sea into a promontory and tidal lagoons, which are a popular habitat for whooper swans.

Page 203

Dettifoss Waterfall, Jökulsá á Fjöllum River, North Thingeyjarsysla District, Iceland

Camera: Hasselblad X Pan II; lens: 30mm f5.6; film: Velvia 50

Jökulsá á Fjöllum flows from the Vatnajökull glacier through a gently sloping plateau, dotted with hyaloclastite mountains and rugged lava fields. Where the land falls away, the current speeds up and the river plunges into the Jökulsá Canyon in a spectacular series of waterfalls, including Dettifoss, Selfoss, Hafragilsfoss and Réttarfoss, without parallel in Iceland.

Page 204-205

Icebergs, Denmark Strait, East Greenland

Camera: Hasselblad X Pan II; lens: 30mm f5.6; film: Velvia 50

Originating in the Arctic Ocean, the East Greenland Current brings cold, low-salinity water southbound along the East Coast of Greenland. It is one of the five main currents that make up the sub-polar gyre, providing a major outflow of cold Arctic waters into the Atlantic Ocean. Rising temperatures and additional fresh water through ice melt could impact on the circulation of currents and affect regional climate.

Page 206

Icebergs, Denmark Strait, East Greenland

Camera: Canon EOS1Ds Mark II; lens: 24–70mm f2.8L IS ISO 100

Icebergs are composed predominantly of fresh water – when water freezes the complex crystal structure of ice does not provide any space for the salt to be incorporated. Icebergs form when large fragments of ice are carved from glaciers or land-based ice sheets that have accumulated from compacted snowfall, often over hundreds of years.

Page 207

Icebergs, Denmark Strait, East Greenland

Camera: Canon EOS1Ds Mark II; lens: 70–200mm f2.8L IS ISO 100

Rising temperatures are likely to cause the melting of at least half the Arctic sea ice by the end of the century. A significant portion of the Greenland ice sheet, which contains enough water to raise the worldwide sea level by about seven metres (23ft), would also melt. Should the Arctic become ice-free in summer, it is likely that polar bears and some seal species would become extinct.

Page 208

Humpback whale, Denmark Strait, East Greenland

Camera: Canon EOS1Ds Mark II; lens: 70–200mm f2.8L IS ISO 100

Backlit by the morning sun, a humpback blows a double stream of spray that rises three to four metres (10–12ft) above the surface of the water. Humpback whales breathe air at the surface through two blowholes located near the top of the head, and their exhalation of warm carbon dioxide is visually enhanced by the cool air temperature over the sea.

Page 209

Humpback whale, Denmark Strait, East Greenland

Camera: Canon EOS1Ds Mark II; lens: 70–200mm f2.8L IS ISO 100

Cetaceans reliant upon ice habitats, including many baleen species that migrate to the poles to feed, will be particularly susceptible to climate change, as polar areas are predicted to experience the greatest temperature changes. Various studies show that the Arctic is undergoing large-scale warming, and that in the last thirty years or so sea ice has decreased in thickness by around 40 per cent.

Page 210

Icebergs, Denmark Strait, East Greenland

Camera: Canon EOS1Ds Mark II; lens: 70–200mm f2.8L IS ISO 100

Melting of the Arctic sea ice will mean that less solar energy is reflected back into space, and instead it will be absorbed by the ocean. The warmer water will melt more sea ice, and eventually the warmer atmosphere will melt more of the ice sheets on Greenland. Since sea ice and sheet ice both consist of fresh water, the result will be a huge increase of fresh water in the Arctic Ocean.

Page 211

Polar ice, Denmark Strait, East Greenland

Camera: Canon EOS1Ds Mark II; lens: 70–200mm f2.8L IS ISO 100

With its high surface current velocities, the East Greenland Current (EGC) carries polar ice and water out of the Arctic Ocean through Fram Strait. In addition to the cold, low-salinity surface water from the Greenland Sea, the EGC is fed by warm, saline water from the south via the Norwegian Atlantic Current, which destabilizes the water column and suppresses ice formation.

Page 212-213

Icetoppen (1,990m), Sondre Skjoldungen Sund, East Greenland

Camera: Hasselblad X Pan II; lens: 30mm f5.6; film: Velvia 50

The aptly named Icetoppen has permanent snow on the summit, but this may change with rising temperatures. Glaciers throughout Greenland are moving faster and shrinking dramatically. As ice melts, water reaches the interface between ice and bedrock, creating a lubricant that allows the ice sheet to slide faster towards the sea.

Page 214

Angiseeq, Sondre Skjoldungen Sund, East Greenland

Camera: Canon EOS1Ds Mark II; lens: 70–200mm f2.8L IS ISO 100

Dwarfed by huge glaciers, our boat, Angiseeq, named after our skipper's grandfather, searches for a snagged anchor. Travelling flat out at five knots, the fifty-year-old boat gave the impression of living in a bygone era and so slowed down the pace of life. It also rewarded us with excellent opportunities to observe wildlife, including humpback whales and bearded seals.

Page 215

Tvillingtoppe (1,410 & 1,541m), Sondre Skjoldungen Sund, East Greenland

Camera: Canon EOS1Ds Mark II; lens: 70–200mm f2.8L IS ISO 100

In the Lakseelven, at the head of Skjoldungen Sund, the Inuit crew caught over thirty salmon in gill nets. Most modern salmonidae species evolved during the geologically recent ice ages, the main reason they prefer cold, clear water. Some scientists are concerned that climate change and rising water temperature could be a threat to salmon and other members of salmonidae.

Page 216

Fata Morgana, Denmark Strait, East Greenland

Camera: Canon EOS1Ds Mark II; lens: 70–200mm f2.8L IS ISO 100

The Fata Morgana mirage occurs where there are alternating warm and cold layers of air near the water surface. Instead of travelling straight through these layers, light is bent towards the colder, denser, air. The result can be a complicated light path that sometimes gives the impression of a castle half in the air and half in the sea. It is named after the fairy shape-shifter Fata Morgana (Morgan le Fay).

Page 217

Icebergs, Denmark Strait, East Greenland

Camera: Canon EOS1Ds Mark II; lens: 70–200mm f2.8L IS ISO 100

Compared with areas of identical latitude, the climate on the southeast coast is colder, owing to the East Greenland current, which carries large amounts of cold Arctic water with sea ice and icebergs southwards along the coast. The region is highly influenced by the proximity of the ice sheet and nunataqs are abundant as well as areas where the ice sheet meets the sea.

WILDERNESS AREAS

The wildernesses featured in this volume are shown on the map opposite. The numbers refer to the pages on which photographs appear.

A full listing of wilderness areas of the world, as identified by Conservation International, is below. By definition, these areas retain 70 per cent or more of their original vegetation, cover at least 10,000 sq km (3,860 sq miles) each, and contain fewer than five people per square kilometre outside of urban areas. Also included in the list are six regions (Appalachians, European Mountains, Sudd, Serengeti, Caatinga, Coastal Deserts of Peru and Chile) which came near to matching but did not fully reach these thresholds.

AFRICA

Serengeti
Kenya, Tanzania

Miombo-Mopane Woodlands and Grasslands
Angola, Botswana, Democratic Republic of the Congo, Malawi, Mozambique, Namibia, South Africa, Tanzania, Zambia, Zimbabwe

Kalahari Desert
Botswana, Namibia, South Africa

Namib Desert
Angola, Namibia

Okavango
Botswana, Namibia

Congo Forests of Central Africa
Angola, Cameroon, Central African Republic, Democratic Republic of the Congo, Equatorial Guinea, Gabon, Republic of Congo

Sudd
Sudan

Sahara/Sahel
Algeria, Burkina Faso, Cameroon, Central African Republic, Chad, Egypt, Eritrea, Ethiopia, Jordan, Libya, Mali, Mauritania, Morocco, Niger, Nigeria, Senegal, Sudan, Tunisia, Western Sahara

ASIA

Central Asian Deserts
Afghanistan, Bangladesh, China, Iran, Kazakhstan, Kyrgyzstan, Mongolia, Pakistan, Russia, Tajikistan, Turkmenistan, Uzbekistan

New Guinea
Papua or Irian Jaya (Indonesia), Papua New Guinea

Sundarbans
Bangladesh, India

Arabian Deserts
Egypt, Iran, Iraq, Israel, Jordan, Kuwait, Oman, Saudi Arabia, Syria, United Arab Emirates, Yemen

AUSTRALASIA

Kimberley
Western Australia

Arnhem Land
North Australia

Australian Deserts
Australia

Cape York
Queensland

Tasmania

SOUTH AMERICA

Patagonia
Argentina, Chile, Falkland Islands

Magellanic Subpolar Rainforests
Argentina, Chile

Bañados del Este
Uruguay

Coastal Deserts of Peru and Chile
Chile, Peru

Chaco
Argentina, Bolivia, Paraguay

Pantanal
Bolivia, Brazil, Paraguay

Caatinga
Brazil

Amazonia
Bolivia, Brazil, Colombia, Ecuador, French Guiana, Guyana, Peru, Suriname, Venezuela

Llanos
Colombia, Venezuela

NORTH AMERICA

Pacific Northwest
Alaska, Canada

North American Boreal Forests
Alaska, Canada

Northern Rocky Mountains
Canada, Idaho, Montana, Washington, Wyoming

Appalachians
Canada, Alabama, Connecticut, Georgia, Kentucky, Maine, Massachusetts, Michigan, New Hampshire, New York, North Carolina, Ohio, Pennsylvania, South Carolina, Tennessee, Vermont, Virginia, West Virginia

Mojave Desert
Arizona, California, Nevada, Utah

Colorado Plateau
Arizona, Colorado, New Mexico, Utah

Baja Californian and Sonoran Deserts
Arizona, California, Mexico

Greater Chihuahuan Desert
Arizona, New Mexico, Texas, Mexico

EUROPE

European Mountains
Albania, Austria, Bosnia-Herzegovina, Bulgaria, Czech Republic, France, Germany, Greece, Italy, Macedonia, Poland, Romania, Slovakia, Slovenia, Spain, Switzerland, Ukraine, United Kingdom, Yugoslavia

European Boreal Forests
Finland, Iceland, Norway, Russia, Sweden

POLAR REGIONS

Arctic Tundra
Alaska, Canada, Finland, Greenland, Iceland, Norway, Russia, Sweden

Antarctica

ARCTIC

150-165
Alaska

196-203
Iceland

184-187
Norway

204-217
Greenland

188-195
Scotland

ASIA

NORTH
AMERICA

ATLANTIC OCEAN

EUROPE

52-61
Pakistan

72-73
Ladakh

174-177
Utah

166-173, 178-179
Arizona

46-47
Tunisia

84-88
Japan

146
Belize

142-145
Venezuela

AFRICA

62-71
Nepal

74-80
Thailand

82-83
Philippines

PACIFIC
OCEAN

SOUTH
AMERICA

14-15, 17-21
Kenya

29-31
Tanzania

40-45
Seychelles

PACIFIC
OCEAN

16
Kenya

INDIAN
OCEAN

81
Indonesia

138-141
Chile

32-39
Namibia

22-28
Zimbabwe

94-99
Western Australia

AUSTRALASIA

136-137
Argentina

100-107
South Australia

SOUTHERN OCEAN

108-123
New Zealand

128-135
Chile

ANTARCTICA

NOTE ON THE PHOTOGRAPHY

Having just celebrated my twenty-fifth year as a professional photographer, I feel that I have come full circle.

My early career started with 35mm Nikon cameras. The legendary Nikon F2AS, with its Photomic head, was then the benchmark among the world's top photojournalists, many of whom were shooting with Kodachrome 64. Soon though, I learnt that creative directors and art buyers didn't share my enthusiasm for the 35mm format, because of its perceived failure to deliver reproduction quality in print: they specified 5 x 4 or 6 x 7 film formats. I next chose to work with a Hasselblad – despite its square format – for the quality of the Carl Zeiss lenses, which were among some of the finest available, giving superb definition, contrast and colour saturation. However, I wrestled with the format and found myself frequently cropping panoramic images from the middle sections of the square transparencies (ironically what the X-Pan effectively did on 35mm film), so when I heard in 1989 that Linhof had re-engineered the Technorama, previously discontinued, I ensured that I had the first camera that arrived in Britain.

During the next four years, I spent my time creating a unique collection of panoramic images of the Scottish Highlands and Islands with the distinctive 6 x 17 format. By the time my first book, *Highland Wilderness*, was published in 1993 by Constable, Fuji had introduced a re-designed GX617 panoramic camera, which featured interchangeable lenses, including 90, 105, 180 and 300mm. This camera, superior in every way, raised the benchmark in panoramic photography, and I immediately began working with it. It was put to good use during the next five years on a second Scottish volume, *Scotland: The Wild Places*, first published by Constable in 2001, and featuring a collection of images captured over the cycle between the solstices and equinoxes.

I had a bigger aim, however: to extend what had worked so successfully in Scotland to the world's wild places and to bring together a collection reflecting the unique ecosystems of the five continents. Since my earliest trips in 1991, I have systematically worked my way around the world, capturing images in some of the world's most extreme environments.

Just over a year ago, I began working digitally with the formidable Canon 1Ds Mark II. The combination of file size and firepower, together with the positive attributes of a 35mm camera, creates a potent cocktail for photography in wild places. For the first time in my career, I feel liberated to concentrate on the concepts of my work, rather than continually to have to debate which camera system is the most suited to any particular assignment – in this respect, I'm back where I started with a 35mm camera, but now with

the reproduction quality equivalent to a 6 x 7. We must accept that camera size and format no longer restrict a photographer's work. Indeed, the period in history in which people have recorded and continue to record images on film has now been defined.

This volume, then, features a range of formats, including images captured on 35mm Canon film cameras, and panoramas photographed with the Fuji GX617, the Linhof Technorama 617S and the superb but short-lived Hasselblad X-Pan II. A small selection of images was shot with a 5 x 4 Ebony 45SU field camera, and the recent digital images were captured on the Canon 1Ds Mark II. In this sense, the portfolio can be viewed as a retrospective of my work.

The panoramic format remains for me the ultimate visual statement able to capture the essence of wild places. Recently, however, I have been concentrating on more intimate aspects of the landscape, including wildlife and images that I describe as 'visual poetry'. As a conservationist and photographer, I see myself as a conduit to the natural world, with the ability to discover nuggets that may subliminally influence the way people think about specific issues. This is a great privilege and one of the reasons why photography has remained such a powerful force in my life – as someone said, 'You don't practise photography – you live it.'

Our contemporary challenge is a great one: how do we address the problems of conserving the ecosystems of this planet while supporting a global population of 6.5 billion people, with an ever-increasing consumption of natural resources? There is no easy answer and the prospects of survival for many species are not good. It will take considerable effort to reverse the ongoing degradation of natural ecosystems and to ensure that their unique biodiversity is protected. Photography alone of course will not solve the problem, but I believe it can play a vital role by rendering the natural world in a language that can be understood by a wider audience, and in the process heightening awareness of some of the issues affecting our planet.

I will leave you with this poignant quotation by the American novelist Wallace Stegner:

We are the most dangerous species of life on the planet, and every other species, including the earth itself, has cause to fear our power to exterminate. But we are also the only species which, when it chooses to do so, will go to great effort to save what it might destroy.

Colin Prior

ACKNOWLEDGEMENTS

Firstly, I am indebted to Geraldine, my wife, for her enduring patience and support during the years I worked on this project. While it was not always possible for me to be around, she has been a steadfast influence in the lives of our two children, Alexandra and Laurence.

I would also like to acknowledge the contribution that my father, Hugh, made to this book. Time spent in wild places, under canvas or in some grim motel on the edge of nowhere has helped us develop a special relationship. I am grateful to him for his unfailing energy, which has helped me capture dramatic images in Nepal, Pakistan, India, Patagonia, Australia and Scotland.

Throughout the duration of this project, I have also been indebted to many individuals who helped me achieve the images that appear here:

Canon (UK) Ltd

Apple

Hasselblad (UK) Ltd

Graham Rutherford, Fuji Film (UK) Ltd

Julie Hanley, Lowepro

Robert White Photographic Ltd

Tim Greening, KE Adventure Travel Ltd

Bob MacDonald, Graham Tiso Ltd

Tony Hook, Abercrombie and Kent Ltd

Chris Holt, British Airways

Karl Ammann, Nanyuki, Kenya

Rob Macdonald, Induna Lodge, Bulawayo, Zimbabwe

Jan Groebler, Windhoek, Namibia

Adrian Skerret, Mahe, Seychelles

Haji Muhammad Iqbal, Baltistan Tours, Islamabad

Bikrum Vikram, Himex Nepal, Kathmandu, Nepal

Mariko Takahashi, Kamakura City, Japan

Rolan Ruoss, Sea Hawk Air Inc, Kodiak Island, Alaska

Neil & Gordon Birnie, Wilderness Scotland, Edinburgh, Scotland

Lynne Bunney, Kimberley Specialists, Kununurra, Western Australia

Department of Conservation and Land Management, Kununurra, WA

Department of Environment and Heritage, Adelaide, South Australia

Bob Jones, New Zealand Photographic Society, Auckland, New Zealand

Graham Dainty, Te Anau, New Zealand

Southern Lakes Helicopters, Te Anau, New Zealand

David Oswin Expeditions, Carlisle, England

Hans Christian Florian Sørensen, Nansen Adventures, Greenland

Dr Ian Player, Wilderness Foundation, South Africa

Vance Martin, Wild Foundation, California

Cristina Mittermeier, International League of Conservation Photographers

Jo Roberts, Wilderness Foundation, Chelmsford, England

Cameron McNeish, TGO Magazine

A special thanks to all those guides, drivers and individuals whom I am unable to name in person but whose contribution to this project was in its own way crucial.

I would also like to thank Mandy McDougall for the overall design concept and book layout, which has been pivotal to its success. Mandy and I have worked together for many years and acknowledge the same fundamental ethos in design – 'less is more.'

Finally, I would like to pay tribute to the support and commitment of the team at Constable & Robinson, particularly to Pete Duncan and Nova Jayne Heath.

 International League of Conservation Photographers

For further information about the work of Colin Prior, contact www.colinprior.co.uk